HeARTwork

✔ S0-AGG-415

HeARTwork

Kiyomi Holland

MILL CITY PRESS

Mill City Press, Inc.
2301 Lucien Way #415
Maitland, FL 32751
407.339.4217
www.millcitypress.net

© 2019 by Kiyomi Holland

All rights reserved. No part of this publication may be reproduced, stored in a retrieval system, or transmitted, in any form or by any means, electronic, mechanical, photocopying, recording, or otherwise, without the prior written permission of the author.

Printed in the United States of America

ISBN-13: 978-1-5456-7223-5

For my family, my children, to all of you who read this, and the future

♥ Acknowledgments ♥

Going through this process was only an idea, a dream. These next people are ones who completely made this a reality and worked so hard to make this come to life.

Brandye Brixius, I cannot thank you enough for starting this project and creating the first steps for everyone to make it what it has become. Thank you for pushing this through, but in reality, you pushed me to see that this wasn't just an idea anymore.

I have to acknowledge, Alexandria Zaldivar. THANK YOU! Every time we talked, it was always good news and it's always good to hear good news! I cannot believe how quickly and seamlessly you put things together. I don't even know if you're real, at this point, because of how incredible you are. You're fabulous. Make sure to tell Kaaren that.

Although I didn't get to talk with either of you, Valerie Willis and Amanda Wright, you guys like to play hide and seek behind the scenes. Amanda, your cover design was as if you had already seen what I had envisioned. What you created became real for me. As soon as I saw it, I was speechless. Valerie, you are the cake to Amanda's frosting! You create the most beautiful interior while Amanda makes everything look enticing. Valerie, I couldn't have asked for something as beautiful as you created. With both of you coming together, you made this book how it is. I cannot thank either of you enough for the vision you both saw without knowing me in the slightest.

Lastly, Sean at the office. Keep yelling in victory!

You are all amazing people that I never thought I would have such a pleasure of working with. Since going through this process, I understand why a team of people is needed, but I never dreamed you were the people, specifically, I needed to have. You are all a part of this heartwork. In life and in the work you do. Not just for me, but for all of those you work so hard for. Thank you all, again. Acknowledging you was the VERY least I could do.

❤ Prologue ❤

The cover photo is a picture I took of play-doh hearts each of my children made. I love those hearts not only because it was sweet, but because each heart is made of combined colors and cracks. To me, it represents how our hearts are made through life experiences. It's definitely not perfect and it's not about having the colors blend seamlessly and gradually together. Everything we go through comes together in a beautiful chaos which makes us unique. Sure, it may be broken into pieces at times, but each piece can be put into a place to create the art of our heart. It is what will make our hearts work.

I had an idea of wanting to write a book for a while but I hesitated mainly because I didn't want it to just be something that was a one way chat. I really wanted this book to be a dialogue between the two of us. So, I'm seeing this book as a conversation, perhaps a story, but mostly, a heart to heart. This may, at times, seem like a journal but that's only because I want to see us as friends, where I can speak completely open and honest with you. I want to be able to bare my soul and my deepest thoughts.

HeARTwork

In this book, I'm going to be raw, and most of all, I'm going to be me. There may be curse words and if you're by offended that, this may not be the book for you. However, I do hope you give it, and me, a chance. There will be tears and laughter, from my end, while writing this. I don't know about from yours, but if it happens, I hope it's for something important that moved you. I will reveal my hopes and dreams. I will share epiphanies that will instantly come to me, as if we are sitting down together. I will reveal secrets, I'm sure. I'm nervous and excited to see where this leads.

I don't want this conversation to be something preached to you. It's about feelings and thoughts that I've felt and learned along my journey, how it led to now, and a reason to remember it all. Believe me; it's not an autobiography from birth. Although, being alive has had a significant impact in all of this, obviously.

February 8th, 2018 is *THE* date. This is the date that made me want to document anything and everything I could think of. However, we will start from the beginning of how it actually began, April 24th, 2015; just a few short, but long, years ago and I'm praying doesn't end before this is finished sharing it with you. I know that sounds dreary to say, however, keep reading and you'll understand why I felt it was important to word it this way.

We all live in a day, in only a moment. It's the only thing we can do for certain. Every moment in that day will impact what happens in the future, even within seconds from then. There are differences in certain dates and moments that stand out amongst others.

Prologue

We can remember the date, time, place, smells, happiness, or guilt. Those significant dates in our lives are the ones we feel have impacted us the most. Take this second to recall the first moment that comes to mind. I'm sure you can recall numerous moments in your timeline given anymore than a second. Your moment may be a lesson, a happy memory, a life changing memory, or even just a recent one. My large, significant, moment is what has driven me to this point. It's what has driven me to talk to you.

Throughout my story I will have a short page, between chapters, about someone who is Happy, Beautiful, and Wealthy (the meaning behind those words, I will explain much later). The questions they were given to answer were questions I've written and given to them. These people are included in our little group of real talk since this isn't just a story of what I've gone through. Everyone should be included.

If you'd like, take this all in as a self exploratory of how you determine what is beautiful to you, how you perceive kindness to be, what you feel you could do for someone, and how you choose to remember your own life. At the end of this journey, think about what impacted you the most to make you wonder, dream, inspire, or change. My hope, more than ANYTHING, is this book inspires you to know YOU are wonderful and good enough. You are worthy of every good thing you receive, no matter how much you think Karma is going to come and bite you so hard in the ass. Yes, I said ass. Raw remember? If you haven't run by now with a "bad" word, then thanks for sticking around.

Before we jump into the Delorean and travel to the past of April 24th, the beginning, I want to share something I've written. It resonates with me each time I read it. It may not hold any significance for you the way it does for me, but it has shaped the way I can view my world, my moments.

"Love and Hate can both change the world. Love spreads, as does hate. But Love will thrive, where hate can't survive." Love, is what has inspired me to start. Love is, usually, what we seek in dark times. I hope the love I've experienced through my life will show how I've grown or, at least, how I plan to keep going and growing. Life, its broken pieces, and the love throughout, has made an art work on my heart.

Here we go. Are you ready? I have some sweaty palms and my heart is racing just a bit faster now. Okay, Kiyomi. No turning back. Just go.

❤ 1 ❤

Let's begin

I was looking at the word, Chapter, and it just doesn't feel right in this story. Mainly because, like I said, this is going to be much different for us. I didn't see "chapter" as a conversation starter.

Imagine we are at a coffee shop together and I started out our conversation as "Chapter 1". DUN DUN DUUUN! Unless I was actually trying to be witty and make you laugh, forget it. So, I will number them and I'll recollect throughout the book as their titled name. For example, I'd recollect this as "Let's Begin".

Here we go. The day the whole story began. April 24th, 2015, started out just like any other day. I was with my husband and my kids. We had gotten a friend's daughter, who feels more like a daughter to me, after school that day and was going to stay the weekend with us. We all joked around and were giddy with being able to spend time together. I cooked dinner and the house filled with the smell of mouth watering home burritos. By 9 p.m., I had started to feel a little strange. I felt like I was starting to feel sick to my stomach, but not enough for me to feel very concerned. I thought maybe the burritos hadn't sat right. I told everyone that I was going to turn in a little early so that I could lie down, hoping that I wasn't coming down with a stomach bug.

From 9 pm on the 24th, to 3am the 25th, were the six hours from feeling a little ill, to changing everything that I never knew or would have thought to happen. It changed all future moments in only a few words, "Matt, help me".

I woke at 3am, the wee hours of the morning of April 25th feeling ill, worse than when I had gone to bed. I felt like I was either going to be sick or that I was going to immediately hold my bottom cheeks together until I sat on the toilet. However, in the short distance from my bed to the ensuite bathroom, I felt like my arms became very weak. I was having trouble lifting my lead weighted arms and squeezing my hands into fists. I sat on the toilet, while I had the garbage can in front of me. This was in case both ends started blowing out and need to call a priest for an exorcism. Just then, while on the "throne", the darkness started surrounding inside my eyes as though I was being enclosed. The white bathroom walls, as I stared straight ahead, looked as though they were darkening and tunneling around me. I was sure I was about to see myself transport into another dimension, spiraling down through a black hole.

I immediately yelled for my husband, Matt. I didn't want to fall to the ground without someone knowing that I had even wakened to go into the bathroom. He came in with a panic from being half asleep and had no idea what was happening. As I tried to tell him that I felt ill and felt as if I was going to pass out, I heard myself talk. My words were slurred. I'm allergic to alcohol so I knew that no party happened, to my knowledge. As I tried to move my arms again, I realized they were still not functional. The dark tunnel, which was still enclosing inside of my eyes, made it hard to focus. I imagined my eyes slowly turning completely black.

As soon as Matt saw me slouching more and more from atop of the toilet, he removed me from the bathroom and placed me on the bed. He laid me on my side in case I were to be sick. At that point, I knew something wasn't right. This wasn't the stomach bug, so I slurred to Matt that he needed to call for an ambulance.

The emergency vehicle showed up at our house, while I looked a complete wreck. I mean, ehh-err-um, I looked like a supermodel. My hair and makeup were flawless while wearing a beautiful satin pajama set. Actually, forget the satin, let's go with silk. Picture them with no sleeves, just little straps, and add white lace across my chest down to the hem of the mini night shirt. Imagine the best body you've ever seen in your entire life, and having perfectly manicured nails. Oh, and don't forget that my bodily hair was perfectly shaven with no smell, at all, emanating from my armpits.

Then the blinded eyes, from my impeccable beauty of course, of the emergency crew, checked my vitals, blood sugar, and asked me several questions, which I don't remember. They let me know that they thought it would be best for me to be checked into Emergency to make sure it wasn't anything more serious. I reluctantly went, mainly because I was starting to come out of my trance a little bit. They hoisted me onto the gurney, and of course I was as light as a feather, and slid the gurney into the ambulance.

When we arrived at Emergency, I had actually started to feel embarrassed. I was still on the gurney and passing by all of these rooms where I saw people who were probably very ill. Then there I was, feeling much better while being wheeled in by something that I felt was just not serious anymore, and of course looking absolutely fabulous at 3am.

The nurses checked all of my vitals, poked me with the needle to run lab work, asked about my medical history, and then all of the questions of my symptoms. The doctor came in and decided I should have a CT scan to rule out anything serious, like a brain aneurysm or stroke. I complied and waited for the test.

Once I was out of the CT bubble, I waited for the doctor to come in with the results of my lab work and the CT scan. He came in nearly just after it was completed and told me everything looked fine and they would ready up the discharge papers. I was home by 5am.

I woke up in the afternoon with the haze of the night briefly lingering in my mind, almost like I was prepared to brush it off that day. I went about my business a bit, but in a very slow way. I hadn't checked my phone, since having been asleep through morning and some of the afternoon. Remember, this is still April 25th, only hours after being discharged. When I finally unplugged my phone from the charger to see what action I missed, I noticed I had a voicemail. When I looked at the time stamp from the phone call, I had missed it at 7am, just 2 hours after being home from the hospital. I hadn't had the number memorized in my phone so I wasn't sure who it could be. I pressed the cell phone to my ear, listened to the voicemail, and it had been the doctor who'd treated me. He stated the radiologist had seen a shadow on my CT scan and they wanted to do a repeat scan, except this time with a contrast MRI.

After telling Matt what I'd just heard, I called the number the doctor left me and immediately heard a receptionist answer. I let her know the doctor's name that I'd seen that early morning and the voice message he'd left after I was discharged. Thankfully, he'd left a note in my chart for the MRI, but the receptionist informed me that the MRI machines weren't available for non emergent patients until Monday, the 27th. I made the appointment and waited that entire weekend in angst.

Monday the 27th came and since Matt was scheduled to work, my dad was willing to take me. The irritating part about the situation, I had to check into emergency again. I'm not upset that they had trauma patients before me; I was upset that I couldn't just wait in a waiting room. My dad and I waited in that little room for six hours, and that included the scan time within that six hours. That room could have been used for someone else. The doctor, who had treated me in the early morning hours on the 25th, was again, the one to come back in and tell me that everything looked great. My dad and I left, a little after 3pm, with irritation from being there for so long but also relief that nothing was wrong. It had just been a weird fluke on the scan.

I pulled into my driveway at 4pm after dropping my dad off at home. I began to receive a phone call from that same doctor. With my foot still on the brake in my driveway, he informed me the radiologist saw a mass on the MRI and he had made a referral to a neurosurgeon. I'd be getting a call soon from that office to make the appointment.

My heart and stomach were engulfed first with fury, then rage, disappointment, sadness, and emptiness. I began to figure out how I would tell all of my family. I had just dropped my dad off minutes before getting the news that I was alright and everything looked fine. My dad had surely told my mom by this point, that I was okay. I was able to leave the hospital with the notion I would be able to live my life the way I had been. I thought that night, I was just ill with a weird mysterious stomach bug. If I had never understood the saying before, I did at that moment; Ignorance is bliss. However, I guess I should follow the rest the saying "knowledge is power".

The neurosurgeon's office called me that day before I could call the rest of my family, besides Matt, since he was still working. They told me they could have me in on Thursday to discuss what they found. Just the word "neurosurgeon" and "brain" in a sentence together makes something sick and twisted fill your insides.

Fast forward three days to Thursday the 30th. Matt and I walked through the glass doors to the office of the neurosurgeon that works for the hospital I was referred from. We waited impatiently in the waiting room to be called back into the clinical room to finally talk to the doctor. The man had a complete lack of bedside manner. There was minimal eye contact to either myself or Matt, and his news for us was maybe why he didn't actually want to look at us. I bet he hates delivering bad news to patients. I know I would.

The immediate word "tumor" doesn't give anyone a feeling of anything good. It's a foreign invader trying to take over the world that is your body. It's a parasite that wants to devour anything good in your life and fill it with worry and uncertainty. He informed us that because of the placement of the tumor, he could not determine if it was malignant or benign. He explained how benign tumors usually present themselves on the surface rather than deep down into the brain or skull. His prognosis was that he wanted to wait a few months, see if it spread, then decide to remove it.

Matt and I left the small disinfected room and then out of the clinic's glass doors. There were stairs near the doors to speed down and out of the building where suites with several specialists worked. The suites encompassed the entire inside of the building. I only made it a few steps out of those clinic doors before I sobbed. You know that cry where you feel like you can't stop, you hyperventilate, you don't want to be loud, but you just can't help it? That was the sob I had, along with that twisted gut feeling happening over and over again. The only thing that Matt could do at that point was hold me in his arms. He hugged me and I ugly cried outside of the see-through clinic doors, while other people were walking around us and toward their fate the in order to check-in at the front desk. I knew, without a doubt, people were staring. I couldn't give a shit how ugly I looked at that moment.

The only thing we could think of was to get a second opinion. The second opinion was going to be at our state hospital, even though it was a two hour drive away. They told us they could get us in the following week.

Let's skip forward to the second opinion appointment, since we already know the diagnosis. This time we weren't in some sort of limbo. The second neurosurgeon said almost the same thing as the other surgeon. However, he said he wanted to run a few more tests to see if the tumor was impairing my vision. He explained that the tumor was very near my optic nerve and carotid artery. We followed through with the different specialists he required. I had vision tests, balance tests, more vision tests, more scans and some other tests that I'm probably missing. So when we finally saw him again, it was May, only a few weeks after being diagnosed.

Somewhere in this whole mess of a situation, I had another one of those "episodes", the ones where I feel sick in the middle of the night and lose function of my arms. I became very cold and shivering, but a more aggressive kind of shivering than just being cold. You know that feeling of being in the cold and your teeth chatter uncontrollably without stopping? That was how I felt but it lasted for much longer than I'd ever experienced, and it was not cold in the house. I let all of my doctors know, and they seemed to not think anything of it.

Let's begin

By July, after more follow up tests in June, they all decided that it would be best to remove the tumor since my vision on the right side, the side of the tumor, was unable to see peripherally in the right upper and bottom quadrants. They explained that the surgery would be a craniotomy, since the placement of the tumor was at the center of the base of my skull. After removing part of my skull, they would replace it with a plate of titanium. They explained to me that I would not set off metal detectors or fly up in the magnetic medical machines. Usually they had to shave off the hair where the incision site would be. Instead of allowing someone else to do it, I took some of the only control I had left; I cut my hair into a pixie cut.

September 4th was the day that the surgery would take place. They had closer openings, but I had to work around Matt's schedule in order to get the most time off for him to help me.

♥ 2 ♥

September 4th

I can remember the date of September 4th, 2015, like it was yesterday. I had dropped my kids off with my mom and sister the afternoon before, since we had to leave by 3 in the morning and drive 2 hours to the city of Seattle. We were hoping to get a little sleep before making the drive. I tried to keep myself as positive as I could. I had a five month, anxiety ridden, limbo between being diagnosed in April, being told the surgery was moving forward, and then the surgery date. I've been known to be a very upbeat person. Being upbeat this time was a huge challenge for me. I guess it could be called a test against my will. I was taken hostage, not just by the tumor, but also by the mental challenge of keeping it together.

September 4th, 2015, was the day that Kiyomi, mother of two children, a wife, a daughter, a sister, a niece, a cousin, a friend, became almost a shell of what she once was. I won't say I died a little inside.

I didn't. Even that is a scornful thing to say. I guess, it was just a new adaptation that I needed to learn to accept. I needed to embrace the new life that was coming forward, especially since it was happening that day. I could have opted to say no. However, all I could think about were my kids. Either way, I would have had my head cut open. Possibly my eye removed, if I'd waited long enough. Since they couldn't tell if it was benign or malignant, I wanted the smaller tumor, that hadn't spread, out of my body.

As soon as we got into the hospital, we were placed into a waiting type area. It wasn't a waiting room; it was more like a big hospital room but with the ability to see everything behind the scenes. They started all of their prep work within this giant room. They gave me the best thing I'd ever had in a hospital, which says a lot. I called it the bubble blanket. It blew warm heat into all of these plastic bubble pockets that made up a blanket with all the pockets coming together. Imagine those bubble pop things that arrive in packages, but think of them square and bigger than the size of your hand.

In the giant room, it smelled sterile from the alcohol and was devoid of almost all color. It actually gave off a very depressing vibe. I would have thought they would have had brightly colored walls. Even some sort of wall that had all of the signatures of people who had gone through neurological surgeries. There wasn't. It was all just beige, white and almost like the colorless version of The Wizard of Oz.

All of a sudden, it was time to tell Matt I loved him. I prepared myself to think happy thoughts while being rolled in. I think, through the whole process, I didn't prepare myself for the pain.

"I wasn't prepared for the pain", was what Matt told me I spoke when I came out of the recovery room and into ICU.

The only thing I can remember was in the actual recovery room. I was in the white bed with the bars so you don't fall off onto the, hopefully, disinfected floor. There was a male nurse on my left standing next to me when I awoke and he had told me his name. I had also heard a groggy sound, of which I'm certain, was him explaining everything and that I was okay and waking up. I immediately started crying for him, reaching out for his arm or hand, basically whatever I could grab onto. I was telling him that I loved him over and over as I sobbed. He sweetly held my crazy hand, because I'm sure he experiences it a lot. I was so drugged that I truly thought he was my husband. I cried and cried when he was leaving me in ICU.

I still try to believe that he and I had something special, that I was the only one. *Sigh*.

Once the surgery was complete, they moved me from room to room for a few days. What they told us was the surgery went great with no complications but they had found new cell growth. Once they said I was stable enough, I could go home and mend there. I was limited on what I could do and I should start to feel a bit better within a few weeks, however, to give myself about 2 months.

The pain that I hadn't been prepared for, stayed, stayed, and stayed, and stayed. It still remains. It's the constant reminder, apart from the plate and scar, which has yet to tell me that my suffering is over. The pain just enrages in my head on a daily basis.

Since the surgery, I started to have more of those "episodes", just like the very first one I had which had me looking fabulous in the ambulance at 3 a.m.. They became more and more frequent. It wasn't until March of 2017, that I was having those episodes every single day, all day long. They became more advanced with more severe symptoms and I found that the use of cannabis oil, CBD, was effective in keeping them somewhat at bay until I was able to get into a neurologist.

The neurologist believed I was having some sort of seizure activity. I was then put on seizure medication to try and control the activity and was referred to see an epileptologist; they specialize in seizures. Epileptologists run more specialized tests in order to diagnose you properly and can also prescribe higher doses of seizure medications that neurologists can't. So if you count time, April 2015 through March 2017, when I saw the neurologist, it was nearly two years of undiagnosed seizures. If you can imagine, it became difficult to live a functional, daily life.

By June 2017, I had a prognosis of insular seizures. The reason it was a prognosis, instead of a diagnosis, is the fact that they are extremely hard to actually diagnose. They are not on the outer lobes that can be read with a topical EEG. I was still kept on seizure medication since it was helping with the episodes.

February 8th, 2018 is what this has all led up to.

Kateland

September 4th

I would like to introduce to you, Kateland Russell. She and another person, whom we consider our sister, have been my "block sisters" for more than half my life. I call them my block sisters because our parents built the houses we all grew up in. It was a cul-de-sac, which was the dead end of another circle of houses that we called "around the block". They are my sisters from other misters. We grew up together, played together, had our hearts broken together. The most wonderful thing I've learned about having them in my life, no matter how much truth we speak to each other, it never ends in hatred or anger. Kateland doesn't like to talk about herself in a light where she is painted a good person. I can tell you, she is one of the best. I will love her forever.

1. What was your happiest moment as a child? As an adult?

As a child, how many "parents" I had helping raise me and the two greatest friends that are still my "block" sisters to this date.
So, I guess my happiest moment would be moving here. To the "block".
As an adult, having my two kids. Also, that my brothers and I always come together and stand by each other when needed.

2. What's the most beautiful thing you've ever witnessed? What is the most beautiful thing you could give to someone else?

Most beautiful thing i have ever witnessed is the love and compassion my kids have for others. The most beautiful thing I could give to someone else was really hard coming up with so I had to ask someone else. Kiyomi said that she felt that the most beautiful thing I give is my time, even when I'm exhausted, even when there is "bad blood"; I would still drop everything and do whatever needed to be done for someone because I do it out of love and determination.

3. What makes you feel wealthy in life or love? What could you add to your life that would make you wealthier than you already are?

I feel wealthy when I always hear how wonderful my kids are. Even when I'm feeling like I'm doing everything wrong, it makes me realize I am doing one thing right in life.
What I could add to my life to make it feel wealthier is to give my family the house and property I have always wanted. Another would be to fully take over my mom's house that I grew up in and fix it up.

♥ 3 ♥

February 8th

Now we have caught up to the day that made me want to have this conversation with you and to document my thoughts. I had an appointment, prior to the 8th, with my specialist, the epileptologist, who was going to look over all imaging and schedule us for the "talk". Both my husband and I knew that the future appointment was going to be the one of discussing the possibility to have procedures, or even surgery. It was to be February 8th, 2018.

February 8th, we drove as if we had been forcefully summoned to the epileptologist. She showed us the new information that she discussed with the surgical board and several other colleagues. She pulled up my scans and showed that part of a lobe was shadowed which could indicate damaged brain tissue. This could be causing the seizures and it could potentially spread. Since it is difficult to diagnose, she informed us that I could end up having surgery to remove the part of the lobe. She explained that procedures done prior to the brain surgery would be to test what hemisphere is dominant in my speech and memory. If it came to having the surgery, she explained there was a chance that I could lose some of both.

The information of the possibility of having my speech or memory impacted, made me ill. I sat in that room with myself, my husband Matt, and my two kids. I sat there while the doctor described all of the procedures that could be taking place and how long this period of time would last, or to me, suffer. Still those words of my memory or speech, I couldn't wrap my thoughts around it. Maybe I had already gone since I couldn't gather my thoughts.

I don't think I was listening as productively as I could have been. Instead, I looked around the small space of the examining office, seeing pictures of brains and their explanations, the smell of antiseptic and the constant cool air flow through the vents. Why is it always so much colder in those places? Then my heart began drowning as I looked at my kids. It made me realize even more, that people could be erased. My memory. _My_ memories. **MY** memories. Not being able to remember my kids or husband would be such a heartbreaking feeling that could NEVER be undone. The worst part, I wouldn't even know about it. If I'm reading this after the procedure, everything in that moment changed. What ran through my mind was, we don't get to choose which memories we get to keep. They are stolen from us.

Yes, the brain surgery just 2 years ago was terrifying and I had every second to think about all of the wrong possibilities, and since then, all the joy I've had has been my family. Every hour, every minute, every second, they have been my joy, my job, my laughter, my cries, my crazy, my sane, my emotional, and my love. It's the one constant through all of this, through the all of the pain and unknown that I have had constant love to remind me that I can keep going. Also, it would be great if none of it will happen and I'll still have this story to look back on. Either way, welcome to my journey of learning and life lessons. We will begin the journey with judgment as we work our way through life and death.

♥ 4 ♥

Judgment.

Judgment, I feel, is the one we need to get out of the way the fastest. Not because we should avoid it, rather that we need to *accept it* and then move the. fuck. on.

None of us can say there hasn't been a moment that we haven't said, or thought of, something scrutinizing about another person. It could be making a judgment based on either their race, their religion, who they associated with, how they look, or even as silly as their opinion. Trolls are everywhere, I've noticed. More judgmental things can come to mind, but we will stick to basics.

Somehow, our life seems to take a little road trip, turn off of a cliff, all while we stare out of our window, sit ideally by, and watch ourselves plummet to our *avoidable* mishaps. I feel that most of the judgment I've witnessed or encountered was of race, social status, and how a person represented their self in a situation.

I will completely agree with you that a judgment based on race, is also being prejudice and racist. Let's keep labeling though. We can also make the title of social status into, snob. We could say thug, conceited, asshole or any other word that would fit in the "presented their self" category. Some of those can even be prejudice.

We are all guilty of this. I overheard this conversation while walking in the breezeway of the hospital. I'm calling out myself of the judgment I made, right now! It's embarrassing.

I saw two women, both dressed in long, soft blue, plain dresses that fell nearly to the floor. Below their dresses were socks that I could barely see. They had plain black shoes that resembled boots, but not quite. They had their hair pulled up and back that were completely covered by white caps. They had cardigans covering their arms and no other skin showing other than what was on their faces and hands. They were talking about another woman; we will name her "Victim". She was most likely someone they both knew but were gossiping about Victim in a very cynical tone. One of the women I was observing whispered loudly about how "Victim" had reprimanded her and had snapped in a nasty tone. Not only that, but it hadn't been in a private setting, so it had embarrassed her. The other woman then put in her two cents and my immediate reaction was, these women look very religious and they are gossiping about someone?! GASP! (Imagine me holding my hand to my chest and dramatizing that gasp). How could this be?

I felt badly about my assumptions and how I portrayed them in my head, but in reality, WHO CARES?! It was in my head. I didn't say it out loud! It's not their fault of how I judged them. It's all my issue. I am the one who walked them past thinking that.

Also for future reference, don't stare. Staring at someone different than you just makes things uncomfortable. I can attest to it, I have a white eyebrow and white eyelashes on the right side of my face. I'm about halfway to collecting black and white puppies to make a fur coat. When someone stares at me, especially with no makeup on, I don't ever know if I'm looking super attractive that day, especially of how fabulous we all know I look in an ambulance, or if it's because they see Cruella De'ville walking around in their town and hastily start to hide their animals.

Accept it. What you've just done, in your head, won't change for them most of the time, unless you stared. If you really feel the need to ask someone about their difference, then do it in a tasteful and respectful manner. It's a good opportunity to learn something different. Most of the time, people don't get offended, and if they do, just run for your life.

Lastly, GET OVER IT! In other words, **MOVE ON**! If you haven't hurt someone's feelings and you've kept your Negative Nancy comments to yourself in your own little traveling mind, don't sit there and beat yourself up about it. Your opinion in your head is your own issue. It wasn't there's and you didn't say anything. Move on with your life and just learn from the time when you thought that you knew a stranger top to bottom. That comment is actually literal in my case.

Judgment.

Did the way the women dressed, whom I saw, impact my life in any type of way? No, except for a lesson. Did their discussion hold any meaning or precedence into my life, or for that matter, make any type of sense? No. Did "Victim" become my best friend because this was a "Mean Girl" situation? Heck yes! Just kidding. What do you think my answer really is? NO!

If it does not impact your life, butt out, have a learning moment, and move on. Why hold onto something when you know you'll probably forget about within 24 hours? I kept mine as a lesson in humility and now I'm able to tell you about what happened.

So, at the end of our "judgment day", keep it to yourself. No one wants your gross, verbal, opinions dumped on them. When I say dumped, I mean that everyone has a butthole and an opinion. They both stink like a big load of dump. If you have to, spray some of the "Poo-pourri" before you open your mouth and drown out some of the stench you may end up regretting later. For example, if someone didn't like what stinky opinion I just said, plug your nose.

"Ultracrepidarian: (short definition), Someone who gives opinions on subjects they know nothing about."

MOVING ON....

♥Laura♥

Judgment.

I introduce you, now, to Laura. We met in a some-what unconventional way. Unconventional, is actually how I make a lot of my friends. There had been an online party for one of those 'work from home' parties. She had been in that group and we got to talking a bit. One day, my husband, kids, and I decided to go out to lunch at a family restaurant. She happened to be our waitress. Honestly, I don't remember much of our encounter or how we even began talking and joking. Every time that we went into the restaurant, if she was there, we made sure to always ask for her. That is how Laura ended up in our lives.

1. What's your happiest memory as a child? As an adult?

My happiest memories are things done with my family. Like swimming at my grandparent's and learning to play cribbage as a kid. Or playing in the snow and sledding around. Late nights with bff's and eating too much junk while talking about boys, dancing to boy bands.
As an adult, my happiest memories are doing the same things with my kids. They both love the water now and the 3 yr old would live in the snow if I let him. The baby is not a fan.
Plus, my bff and I still get together and sing to the old boy bands and talk about "boys".

2. What's the most beautiful thing you've ever witnessed? What's the most beautiful thing you can give to another person?

The most beautiful, and disgusting, thing I've ever seen is child birth and those first moments of a mother meeting her little one. I've seen 3 births.
The most beautiful thing I've ever given anyone is 2 precious little boys.

3. What makes you feel wealthy in life or love? What can you add to your life that will make you feel wealthier than you already are?

Love and snuggles make me feel wealthy. When my family is all snuggled up together for a nap or movie I feel like we could never need anything else.
Not going to lie though, filling my giant freezer in the garage would help me feel wealthier. These kids are only 3yrs and 8 months, but wow do they love to eat
In summary: my family, both those related and those chosen, are everything to me.

❤ 5 ❤

Life

I never thought that life, my life, would turn in such a way, that I'd need this much emotional level of support. Sure, there was some definite physical support in the beginning, but the emotional and mental support that I'd need to try and keep going is strength beyond anything I could have imagined. I don't mean just the support of my family, because that is a huge support system if you have it. I also mean the support from myself.

Being engulfed in those demanding "life" moments, no matter what it is, who you are, how severe it is, the support of your own self is what will keep you in the game. It will keep you in the moment of just making it a few seconds longer. My friend sent me something that said, "If the best you can do today is get out of bed, you've hit your goal".

In daily life, I may run into someone in a random place, have them text me, or will hear on my end of the phone receiver, "I don't know how you go through that. I wouldn't be able to be that strong. You are such an inspiration". If you suffer with chronic pain, chronic illness, even an invisible illness that manifests and taxes you to the core, or life just seems to keep handing you shitty deals, you will identify with what was said. While I understand they are coming from a place of love and trying to show that they see your strength, unfortunately they will know that type of defeat soon enough.

There will come a time for everyone to stumble to that crossroads and they'll be hearing the same "strength speech". I'll give you something you can choose to respond with, to those who don't quite understand yet.

"You never know your true strength, until you are at the mercy of your weakness."

That quote, written from my own broken head, was a "midnight write". I have a small journal near my bed. I keep it in case I wake throughout the night and have a thought that pops into my head, and I write it down quickly before I lose it. It's when I'm still mostly lucid to remember my words through my dream state. It's that place where you feel hazed and feel like you can't quite open your eyes all the way. It's the place between woken sanity but still "in" and "feeling" what was just drifting through. The feeling I compare it to be is a whisper. It's like being waist deep in a still summer lake where a hand barely caresses the horizon of the water, barely making a ripple. The feeling of the water reminds me of a cross between silk and velvet. Sometimes, I'll write down that ripple, but because my memory has now been left drifting slowly away in the water, I won't remember that it's in my little journal until sometime much later.

The quote is true for every person. It's a point where something, you feel, is catastrophic and you have no idea how you'll cope. But you do. Time is against you and sometimes all you want is for time to stop for just a moment or you want it to just move forward so that you can pretend to numb yourself.

When I say, "strength at the mercy of your weakness", I picture a stone-faced, large, and dark statue towering over me. It's a likeness to the Lincoln Memorial Statue. The vantage point, at which I see, is from the shoulder of that large and dark statue. I'm on my knees, with my hands in a prayer of pleading, on a white and black checkered marble floor. A vignette encompasses everything, save one filtered light, gleaming from a high yellowed window, directly on me. It barely illuminates any detailed feature of the lofty statue as it peers down on me in superiority. As I imagine myself in that pleading prayer, I'm begging on my knees, I wail for mercy to relieve whatever struggle is surrounding me silently in the darkness. The strength that manifests from that mercy is forcing my feet to stand up in that spotlight, no matter how slowly or painfully I have to do it.

I'll admit, I've followed through with falling back to the floor, on my hands and knees, in tears, and having screamed until I've nearly felt the air disappear from my lungs. I think about having my knees crash to rocky pavement instead of memory foam, just to relieve many of the other anguishes that possess me. These struggles in life can make us feel like we fall into despair and torturous agony. Through all of this, remember that our strength doesn't come from *simply* moving on or getting over it. The strength comes from picking out the large shards of cemented rock that have embedded themselves in our skin, when you were either pleading on your knees or falling back down. It doesn't come from not thinking about the grief devouring our hearts. It's that painful strain to stand.

Although painful at times, my decision and perception about Life won't change. Though it has its strife and knowing its end, Life is wonderful, magical, breathtaking, heartbreaking, demise ridden, risk taking, cherished, merciful, challenging, regretful, and every single moment of Life is worth it. If you make the most of every one of those single moments and single hardships, any memory you've made, or will make, creates the only person in the entire world. You are the only one copy that is unique in every aspect and are the only difference through life to make an unexpected open end just by living and making your ripple in the world. Our lives are worth living, through any scenario of good or bad, to our inevitable expiring.

I feel one of the most important pieces of information I've found on Life is a poem by Max Ehrmann that was written in 1927. This pose poem is called "Desiderata". There was a point in time that I questioned, philosophically, where I was currently with my thoughts and life versus how I inevitably wanted my life to be lived. I was introduced to "Desiderata" by a friend who had gone through something similar, then spoke a line from the poem. I'd say there was a favorite part or a significant phrase in the entire poem that influenced me in a provincial way. However, there isn't one single phrase or paragraph. The entire poem, of the genius, Max Ehramnn, was so moving that I sprang into tears and felt a good weight of pressure hit me as though I'd been living life all wrong, until that point.

"Go placidly amid the noise and the haste, and remember what peace there may be in silence. As far as possible, without surrender, be on good terms with all persons.
Speak your truth quietly and clearly; and listen to others, even to the dull and the ignorant; they too have their story.
Avoid loud and aggressive persons; they are vexatious to the spirit. If you compare yourself with others, you may become vain or bitter, for always there will be greater and lesser persons than yourself.
Enjoy your achievements as well as your plans.
Keep interested in your own career, however humble; it is a real possession in the changing fortunes of time.
Exercise caution in your business affairs, for the world is full of trickery. But let this not blind you to what virtue there is; many persons strive for high ideals, and everywhere life is full of heroism.
Be yourself. Especially do not feign affection.
Neither be cynical about love; for in the face of all aridity and disenchantment it is as perennial as the grass.
Take kindly the counsel of the years, gracefully surrendering the things of youth.

HeARTwork

Nurture strength of spirit to shield you in sudden misfortune. But do not distress yourself with dark imaginings. Many fears are born of fatigue and loneliness.

Beyond a wholesome discipline, be gentle with yourself. You are a child of the universe no less than the trees and the stars; you have a right to be here.

And whether or not it is clear to you, no doubt the universe is unfolding as it should. Therefore be at peace with God, whatever you conceive Him to be. And whatever your labors and aspirations, in the noisy confusion of life, keep peace in your soul. With all its sham, drudgery and broken dreams, it is still a beautiful world. Be cheerful. Strive to be happy."

As this is the end of our chat of Life, I will say, it's so nice to have met you.

"Keep your face to the sunshine, and you cannot see a shadow." –Helen Keller

❤ 6 ❤

Death

While I just sat here and thought about how I would describe the exact feelings I felt about life, my obvious next thought was death. Every single person has an expiration date. Unlike a carton of milk, you just don't know when it is. However, like a carton of milk, you know that no matter what, there will be something foul and sour somewhere in life and you feel like it could as well be death.

My mom has always said we will always be disappointed in the people we love. She said a lot of that is due to the hurt you'll feel when they are no longer here with us. It's when you have something that you want to say and can hear their voice speaking back to you. Instead, you're left with speaking to the open air, with words merging into the wind. Unfortunately, we will all have this disappointment. We will all have that pain that we dread and it will cut us so deep that sometimes just thinking for a split second of them makes your throat lump and the sting of the salt building in your eyes.

"I didn't want to kiss you goodbye, that was the trouble. I wanted to kiss you goodnight; and there's a lot of difference." –Ernest Hemingway

As we all learn, Life is definitely not a movie; it's not even some really good and trashy reality T.V. It's something that you know you'll never understand how it will be played out. We will never understand it but we do know the end outcome. Your perception of death, however it may be, is the inevitable end to any living thing. It won't matter what religion, what God, or what saint or evil life you've led. It's life to death. It's the thing that every person in the entire world has in common. We are held and lifted into life, then enveloped and lowered to the grave.

It's normal for a person to wonder what may come once we die. Some religions, though there are many, have common denominators. We live on this Earth, live a life that is dutiful to the God that is believed in, and then die in a peace where the soul is taken to another realm. Some people have a belief that after death, there becomes *nothing*. Their belief consists of no afterlife and no soul that moves forward after this.

Belief: *noun* 1.An acceptance that a statement is true or that something exists. 2. Trust, faith, or confidence in someone or something.

The definition of belief is blurry from what I've experienced. In certain situations, my belief feels like fact. I'll explain to you why that is.

Remember how I told you I would reveal my deepest secrets? This secret is like trying to see myself as an ant staring up toward the sky into the eyes of a giant. Only my close friends and family, and some people who I have been compelled to talk to, know that I carry this with me. My truth from my belief about death has come from years of an experience that I'd previously denied and fought with.

Let me tell you some stories and how this has led to my truth about death.

The earliest I can remember was age two. Now, some can chalk this up to an age where imagination runs free. While I can agree with that thought, these situations have still continued through my adulthood.

I was with my mom and her friend. We'll call her friend Sally to keep everything anonymous. I don't remember where we had been or what we'd been doing but we went back to Sally's house. She had a kitchen that had a separation, which led into a parlor room. We were all standing in the kitchen, when I looked past the span of it and stared into the parlor. On the opposite wall of where I stood, which paralleled to the kitchen, there sat a chair. When I looked at the chair I could see a figure of a man, dressed all in black, a big hat on his head, and his ankle propped casually on his opposite knee. His head was held slightly down and then slowly raised it to face me. I asked my mom and Sally who the man was that was sitting in her chair. They both looked past the sliding doors into the parlor and said that there was no one there. I repeated saying yes, there's a man sitting right there in the chair while I pointed in that direction. I saw both of them look at each other and I think I remember them asking me what he looked like. As I was talking about him, I showed them with my finger that he had risen from the chair and started walking out of the room.

When I saw him the second time, I was around five years old. We were walking up the stairs to the bedrooms, also where Sally had her sewing room. As we were walking step by step, I had made a comment about how the man didn't even need to use doors because he just walked through a wall.

Now, anyone with a child could obviously say that it's all imaginative. I did learn, when I had grown much older, that the only other person who saw this man was the daughter of Sally. She was a young teenager at the time and would go straight to her room from school, shut her door, and fall to her knees to pray until her mom came home from work. She was very uncomfortable in the home with the presence she would see and feel.

That type of experience never became an isolated incident for me. As a child, I could feel things others couldn't. I could see things others said they couldn't see. I knew things that others didn't know.

A major incident I can remember, where I knew something that a newly six year old wouldn't know, was my biological father dying. I was sitting in front of the television when the phone rang. I didn't know anything at that point. In my mind I said to myself, "That must be the phone call saying that my dad died". My immediate reaction was to forget it since I knew that couldn't be true. However, not long after the phone call came, I was told that he had passed. That thought I'd had was something I felt I could never vocalize to anyone. A six year old child thinking about someone you love dying without knowing any information is, for lack of a better word, odd.

The circumstances became more familiar and with each year it seemed that things would become more prominent or new things would show up. The ultimate familiarity, at the time, was knowing Death. I could feel when Death was coming, or I would have a dream about a person dying, even without seeing them for long periods of time. Although it's hard to comprehend all of it, I feel more prepared before it happens. I wouldn't say it's a blessing, but it helps me to know that I'm not crazy. Not fully anyways.

By my teen years, premonitions would come and sometimes messages from loved ones who had passed would come through for other people. It wasn't frequent, but it was much more than what I was used to with just the death premonitions. I'd also have those "gut" feelings and most of the time I thought I was a really great profiler that had a knack for reading people or knowing something about their future. This became very difficult for me during school years.

When I was 16, 10 years after my father passed, I'd finally had my first real message dream from my dad. I'd never had one from him before so it stands out so much for me. In my dream, my mom and I were standing in our house. The sun was blaring through the sliding glass door and the warmth, and peace, I felt was incredible. A telephone that we'd rid of in real life, since it no longer worked, was sitting on the "dream" phone desk. It began ringing and I answered it.

"Hello?" I said with confusion since I had known the phone didn't work.

"Hey Kiyo!" My dad said.

"Dad? Oh my gosh, I've missed you so much and I love you!"

"How are you doing? How's school?"

"Everything is good, I just miss you so much."

"What are you doing right now?" He asked this in the middle of the conversation.

In this dream, I had walked into my bedroom and saw a box with all of my grandpa's, his dad's, old papers and then at the bottom of the box was some money.

"Oh, I just walked into my room and I found a box full of grandpa's papers and some money at the bottom of the box. I'm just going to leave it there though because it's not meant for me."

All of a sudden, the phone just cut out. I began screaming and crying and just feeling the ache of missing him so much all over again. Then, again, the phone rang, but in my hand. I stopped crying and screaming and answered the phone.

"Hello?"

"Kiyo, knock it off. I love you, but I'm not going to call again. Okay?"

"Okay, I love you too dad."

I went, during that summer, to visit my aunt, my dad's sister, who had boxes full of my grandparent's things. I had told her about my dream a month prior. We were cleaning out the spare room and were slowly going through each box. I opened a box and immediately my breath caught. I started sifting through all of my grandpa's old newspapers and things when I saw my grandmother's purse at the bottom of the box. I opened to check and money fell out of the purse.

Death

Without revealing what I'd found, I asked my aunt if she remembered the dream I had and she said yes. I showed her the money that fell out into my hand. She'd just recently gone through a divorce and had moved everything into a small home in Portland, OR. She was broke most of the time while having just moved there and that money I'd dreamt of had been meant for her.

My dad hasn't called again, or visited me in my dreams. He does send me chickadee birds and feathers. Even the birds have a story behind it that was just between him and me. I believe he's still around me; I just can't get him to come visit me that way that I want.

"In my tears, I swear I hear a whisper.
It feeds a comfort as the warmth of summer then can turn into an ache of winter.
It's funny, I've already said goodbye but I say hello everyday.
I run memories through my mind until I find 'the one' and set it on replay.
I'll smile, maybe a quick sound escapes of what would be a laugh,
Then the somber of this day brings me back to when I saw you last.
There's still part of my heart that grasps the sadness of winter,
But in that part of sadness comes joy, because I swear I hear you whisper."

-Kiyomi Holland

I won't mention the names of the people I've spoken to about their messages I'd received from their loved ones because a lot of it is private. They all know who they are. I do want to share with you only a few tiny examples. I have had a message from a father to his daughter that she wasn't listening to him about something extremely important. In this dream, he was yelling at her and she was refusing to listen by snubbing her face up and had turned her head away from him. She even had her eyes close. It looked like a typical parent and child relationship. There had been some words and messages I was supposed to relay to her. When I awoke from the dream, I immediately called her. I gave her a list of things that were explained to me and the imagery that I saw that I felt was important and to be aware of. I explained that it was going to be a tremendous trial to go through but I didn't see Death. Two months later she was diagnosed with a brain tumor and was having surgery a few days from her initial diagnosis.

Upon waking from receiving a message dream, I will feel immediately compelled to tell the person the message I was given. If I don't do it right away, it will feel like a push of anxiety all day long. I have noticed, when I'm given message dreams, I'm not normally greeted with skepticism. There has been one where she said if she'd not done a specific thing that morning, minutes before me calling, she may have not believed me.

I've given messages from my loved ones to my other loved ones. There have been people whom I haven't talked to in years where I've been given information from their family, ones that have passed, that I have to decipher and give it clearly to them. I've been given peace dreams that were just for me. They were from people I love that have passed away and it's usually when I really need a comfort. I still see "people" sometimes, though I call them energy or spirits. I can feel the energy of whether it's a male or a female and also if the energy is threatening. When I "see" them, it's not like a full on figure that looks like a living person. The best way I can describe how I see them is like a form that looks 3-D from the background. It reminds me of a bubble of water that has spilled onto the alphabet and the letter is slightly magnified.

Matt still has a hard time with me "seeing" things. He used to be very scared of the premonitions, the spirits, and the messages. Now, most of the time he just doesn't want me to say when I see someone standing in the doorframe. He doesn't' mind the premonitions or the dreams and messages I have to give to people anymore. So I do feel supported in my strange ways. Whereas before, I did feel like I had to suppress all of those things and even felt judged when I would say anything about it. I was told that it wasn't real and that what I was experiencing was evil. It was that lack of kindness that sent me into secrecy most of the time.

For me, I honestly can't say how I believe death is, since my definition is a line that most people don't experience. I really don't think we are supposed to understand it. I think that our brains are too "simplistic" to understand the depths of everything, including death. I do believe in an afterlife. I have absolutely no clue as to what it is. I know my truth that I know things that others don't. I know my truth that I get messages that are validated by the people I give them to. I know my truth that I'm not alone in thinking this way or believing in these things. I don't believe I'm evil or possessed. I don't believe I'm insane, although, I do like to be a little form of different sometimes. It's all down to beliefs and self experiences. What do you believe?

"Whether one believes in religion or not, and whether one believes in rebirth or not, there isn't anyone who doesn't appreciate kindness and compassion." – Dalai Lama

♥ 7 ♥

Self Reliance.

There was something I mentioned in the section, "Life", about how you have to rely on your own mental support to get by day to day. This is true for this part of the conversation as well. Through this, you'll read about what I've learned, experienced, and what has resonated with me on my own self reliance journey.

Self reliance is what has kept us alive throughout these years. It's a defense mechanism as well as a survival tactic. We are selfish beings, we can't help it. I am going to repeat this, a lot.

Along with self reliance, comes responsibility. Picture this. You're walking through the store and you pick up everything and anything you've wanted. It doesn't matter if it's a grocery store or the finest wine or clothing shop on 5th Avenue. You then begin to feel something similar to the scene of the movie "Bridesmaids". You start to shart, shit, crack, or break something. You're basically like a bull in a china shop. You look at the mess behind you, and you hurriedly walk off. Congratulations. You just mastered public humiliation; you've left that giant pile of "shit" for someone else to pick up. You were responsible for the mess. So with what I just said, responsibility comes with self reliance.

I didn't call this "Responsibility" for a reason. While you obviously have responsibility in your life, self reliance is the tower, the peak, the king. You rely on yourself (eh, hem...self reliance) to survive and it's your responsibility to help yourself do that. Duh.

The best analogy is of the children's song, "Row Your Boat", which originates back to 1852. Apparently, back then, they had their shit together. If you break down the song, the lyrics become very detailed. You'll notice how this song will trickle through the rest of this book.

The beginning starts out as "Row your boat...".

Take a moment and read that again. Row your boat. Honest time, this was something that I've seriously had to overhaul and learn to do as I'm told. Does that statement say, "your friend's boat"? NO! It says plain as day, YOUR boat. That means that your self reliance will keep you from going crazy, like jumping out of your boat in freezing water. Crawling into someone else's boat only means they are willing to give up their own self reliance and responsibility. It's also adding your lack of self care into the hands of someone else. You're poisoning the waters for yourself and for them. For me, the only person I would allow to come in my boat is my God. Or maybe Dr. Phil if I needed a wake up call.

Self Reliance.

You're in a single person kayak, alone, and free. You're in the middle of a beautiful lake taking in all of the scenery of the greenery that's reflecting on the clear waters. You're making your way through the velvet water with each stroke of your paddle. The peace surrounding you takes your breath away and you wonder why you don't take this kind of break for yourself more often. Suddenly, you see the scary clown from movies, waving slowly at you from the shore. He may even be calling out to you, asking if you can take him somewhere. Don't you dare drag your kayak to that shore. That clown will take your ass down and drown you both, but he'll magically come back to life for his next rowing victim. He doesn't have his own boat, and he never will. You take care of your own. Take care of yourself. Don't let someone drown your kayak and don't take over for someone else's. Let them do what they need to do to work out how to live. Let them figure out their path. Don't tell them what to do. You'll just get pissed off if they don't listen to your obvious logic. Then you'll flip their kayak over while whistling the "Row Your Boat" tune.

The next part of the song, "Gently down the stream…", means don't act like you're about to go through some white water rapids and think you're about to head down a waterfall like the beginning of Pocahontas. Don't be a drama queen. It means GENTLY. Not dramatically, not fast, not chaotic. It means calmly and rationally.

When you row gently, you're allowing yourself to take in everything around you. You're allowing yourself to remain balanced and observant. You're able to see some of the next steps to take. You'll more than likely not sabotage yourself. So stop rowing yourself down Niagara Falls and think about, not only how it will impact your life, but also the lives that you are actually responsible for, like children.

I associate that part of the song to how I had to take every bit of my stream blindfolded but still had to try my best to remain calm. Having my kids helped me to not freak out so much. It helped me to stay within the calm stream, with maybe a few little rocks or boulders here and there. However, keeping a rational head creates a stable being. I was able to take in the information and make the best choices I could with all the chaos and fear going on around me.

What you should be prepared for is this next verse, "Merrily, Merrily, Merrily, Merrily...". Come on you guys, they said it four times. Obviously it's important. I had a hard time accepting this because I was already rowing that damn boat by myself and in a calm freaking stream. Now it says I had to do it with a big giant smile on my face?

You've already been rowing your own boat gently down the stream, not down Niagara Falls, and you're observing all around you. Check your fear level. If you're looking for bears, some sort of a mutant fresh water shark, or even the clown, get Zen. Or should we say merry (Pretend I'm doing a wink face at you.)? This does not mean you're rowing your boat down the stream with your eyes drifting off into different directions like a chameleon, laughing like you're some sort of hyena from "Lion King", while sounding like Mr. Burns from The Simpsons. You're calmly, happily, and peacefully rowing yourself gently through your life. You'll hit a couple of rapids and it is only natural to freak out every once in a while. That's okay, as long as what you hit aren't humans. That, my friend, is called homicide.

"Life is but a dream". Those words were the pivot point when I heard them. Life actually is but a dream. Life is so fleeting. Your brain doesn't actually mature until you're about 25. So when they say, "Young and stupid", it's actually true.

You'll blink and time has passed into another time you never thought you'd come to. When you're young, all you think about is getting to that other milestone. You're 13, you can't wait to be 16. You're 16, you can't wait to be 18. You're 18 and you can't wait to be 21. Once you hit 21, it's like a brick wall. Every milestone birthday after that are cards that say how old you're getting. Thanks so very much Hallmark, for letting us gift loved ones cards of hate!

Life is but a dream. Whenever I hear that, I think of sitting with my kids and a moment happens that I feel like I want to relive in my mind forever. That moment, no matter who remembers it, was from my own point of view. I think about memories being devoured by something so quickly by a slice and dice, and I wish that I'd written everything down. I wish I'd recorded voices and faces more. As I sit hear with tears filling my eyes, I would feel robbed by that simple action.

I've felt robbed of memories before. I get to hear the memories from other people about someone that I didn't get to know as well, but were important in my life. An example would be my dad. I knew him for six years, only as a child, and I can only recall a few certain moments. I can't really see his face, but I can see a face with only certain features, like a beard. I can't remember his voice other than two sentences. It's like a dream. It's like I've woken from a sleep and the realness of it starts to drift slowly away, like a memory of a dream, throughout the day.

I know that everyone will have this feeling of loss. All I want to say to you is, I'm so very sorry. What I can only hope for you, are moments of peace, no matter how long they last.

Row gently and happily down your stream, because life will be gone with blinks, heartbeats, breezes and voices. Whether or not you have a good attitude or an attitude that no one likes to be around, life's dream will still go on. Being self reliant will be your drive to continue your gentle path. Allow your self reliance to preserve yourself, even if the responsible thing is to walk away. If you're walking away from that clown, good choice but stop walking and bloody run!

When you expect, you set up and create disappointment. Rowing on.

♡Taryn♡

HeARTwork

Taryn is another very close friend that I've known for over 10 years. We met in beauty school and she had a resting bitch face like no one I've ever seen. I'm good at reading people though, so I knew there was a good person in there and she just looked so cautiously at everything. She's amazing and funny. She is a fighter and has done everything she can to help her children. I love her so much and her family has become another family for me to love.

1. What was the happiest memory when you were a child?

Most of my happiest memories from childhood are from just hanging out with my siblings and my mom. If I had to choose when I was the happiest, it would be this.. My mom and I had somewhat of a tradition. We had an old wooded swing on our back deck, we would pile blankets up on it. We would cuddle under the blankets for a while drinking our English breakfast tea and snacking on tea cookies. I'm not sure what we talked about or if there was anything more to it, I just felt so special to be sitting there with my mom.

What's the happiest memory as an adult?

As an adult, I think we definitely make our own happiness. I could choose lots of memories for this, the birth of my kids, finishing school, ect.. But, my happiest memory is also one of my saddest. My mom got married over a year ago now, in Mexico. We weren't in a good place with our relationship. It was my fault. I wasn't in a good place with my life, I pushed everyone away. I did a lot of damage. But, I wanted to go, I wanted to celebrate their happiness. Her husband is the man I consider to be my dad. I was so ridiculously happy for them! With the situation I was in, I wasn't able to go. My mom has impacted my life in a lot of ways. Her and her husband have so much love for each other. They spent 10 years together before they married. Missing their wedding was definitely a huge wake up call for me. It made me realize what I have been lacking and the changes that I needed to make for myself and my children. Which is the happiest memory. Having my family and my kids together all in the same room. That is happiness.

2. What was the most beautiful thing you've ever witnessed?

The most beautiful thing I've witnessed? That's hard. In my opinion, we have beauty surrounding us every day. You just have to notice it. I think watching my kids grow is the most beautiful. Their personalities, humor, and imaginations. Seeing their problem solving skills grow, while being proud of them for their learning capabilities. They are amazing creatures. Sometimes when I sit back and watch them, their love for each other and beauty within them makes me cry.

What's the most beautiful thing you could give to someone else?

Time. Your time is the most important thing. I have seen both sides of this. From feeling like no one in the world had a moment for you, to being the one so caught up in something that others around you feel invisible. A moment of your time can go a long way to helping someone else.

3. What makes you feel wealthy in life?

My friends and family. I have this support system that I overlooked for a long time out of pride and stubbornness. I have love, happiness, and support. These people have given me endless love and their time. That makes me feel wealthy.

What could you do that would make you feel even more wealthy?

This one is hard. My life has changed so much over the last year that it's hard for me to think of something. The selfish side would like me to say I wish I didn't have to share my kids. I wish I had a better job. I wish I could sit at home and talk to my best friend all day. Lol, honestly, my true answer would be to work on myself. To remember to give my time. To not speak harshly, to give my love more freely. To remember that everyone loves differently.

♥ 8 ♥

Individuality

Every person is different. Every person has their own boat and their own way of living. Everyone has their own quirks, their own speech, and their own thoughts. As much as we would love to be mind readers sometimes, this is all what makes us individuals.

When I would hear that word, individual, I just thought of a person, no one in particular, just a noun. It was usually how we spoke about people in groups in school or words in a textbook. Just a "one size fits all" type of word. The really sad thing when I think about trying to be an individual was that I actually had wanted to be like everyone else, be included and be part of the grouped crowd. I didn't want to stand out; I didn't want to be different. Now that I'm an adult, when I say individual, it makes me think unique. It makes me see individual as an adjective. We each have very different qualities.

HeARTwork

I have some really great friends, and we are so alike, but even still, very opposite. We are individual. Singular. There are things in us that single us out amongst the entire world! The ENTIRE world! It's so hard to wrap my mind around thoughts like this.

The first thing that comes to my mind about individuality is the song by Rick Nelson, called "Garden Party". The chorus goes:

"But it's alright now,

I learned my lesson well.

You see, ya' can't please everyone so,

Ya' got to please yourself."

I wish that the last line had been, "You've got to be yourself", because it would have been much more fitting to this. However, I couldn't get into his mind and make him change it. He was an individual and thought of the song, how he saw fit. He's right. You can't please everyone in this world.

During highschool, Harry Potter had already taken over. One of my friends had been a huge fan from the beginning, before they'd even made it a movie. There was a day my friend decided to wear some Harry Potter glasses to school. They had no lenses, they were just round, black, spectacles that had no purpose other than that she liked them. Our teacher, whom I still love dearly, asked her to remove the glasses. She told him no. He repeated himself and then said that if she didn't take them off, she'd be sent out of class and to the principal's office. She blatantly said no, again. He asked her to leave the room, and the fierceness I saw come over her was sheer brilliance. It was terrifying but so inspiring. As she stormed right out of that room with her arms flying and the bottom of her long shirt looking, fittingly, like a cape, she spat out, "I don't need to take these glasses off, prescription or not. I'm expressing my individuality!" At that moment, I knew we'd be friends forever.

I was too scared to do anything too "individual". Now that I'm older, I express it like a skunk sprays, full and potent. You can't please everyone. Just make sure you're happy being yourself. That's the best thing you can always be. Just be yourself. There is no better version of you. You are the only "you" in the world, the entire world. I was just deep in thought about individuality, I don't want to miss anything. I'm alone in the dark writing on my laptop, which seems to be a common occurrence, and I thought about what could scare me about individuality. My immediate reaction was that of panic, I could be a sheep! Not asleep and not like a literal "BAAAA" sheep, I mean a sheep-ole (sheep+people). Being a sheep would be awful for me because I like being different, but then I started to think about the people who just want to be sheep. Are there such things? The only explanation I could think of was that they've been so out of place their whole lives that they just want to fit in. They want to be accepted and treated like a person. Saying this makes me very sad. How terrible to be in a life where you just want to be accepted and crave it, all because you've been used to being different. If this is you reading right now, an individual needing appreciation and affirmation, only to have the chair kicked out from underneath you, I'm so sorry. I'm so very sorry that you've just wanted to be treated respectfully, to feel like you're included, or that you aren't weird. Different is a good thing and remember, you deserve any good thing that comes to you. Value your difference, and if you can, make it even better. If no one else can support you, I hope I can.

I guess, this book is expressing my individuality. So, if you need lens less glasses to keep seeing what I have to say, put them on. Even if you have to squiggle a little lightning bolt to your head before doing it, be my guest. Now that's a horse of a different color (wink face).

"I'd rather be a freak than a clone." –Joanne Harris

Alohomora, we'll unlock the door to the next chapter. POOF!

❤ 9 ❤

Vulnerability and The Naked Years

I have a list of things to choose as chapters, so I can discuss them with you, listed on a notepad. I have looked over the list, added to the list, scattered the list, until I felt like I could put my computer in front of me again. I had no idea where to start after individuality. Then, I looked at one of the words I listed, and I stared at it, almost like it was a completely new word to me. When it finally came into my eyes and somehow reached the parts of my brain that were able to process the words I see and decipher, which is very few and far between lately, I knew it was the perfect way to move forward.

Vulnerability.

Vulnerability can start at any age, mainly because it's also something that can be so life changing to anyone. I felt that this topic was suitable since we just went over individuality and how being different is sometimes scary.

Teenage years are usually the notorious times in our lives where we constantly wonder what people think about us. We sit there and scrutinize everything in our mind we could say out loud that would make us sound cool or to fit in better with the people you think of as friends. Yep, teenage years are what we adults should now call, "The Naked Years".

Forget about the "Wonder Years". In the show, they go through their teenage awkward years, but they didn't really get to show ALL of the ugly experiences and reactions in a television series. Now I can see where they get the title "Wonder" from because you go through the whole teenage thing, "wondering" when you're going to get out of it. Especially because you'll go through junior and high school feeling like you'll be eaten alive.

For me, the age of "kids will be kids" ended the year of going into junior high. Once you get into the pubescent scent that will make your nostrils flare of all of the smells that WERE NOT there the year before, it's like you are expected to become a more mature version of yourself when you're barely 13. All you hear about is who is going out with who, which teacher you hate the most, who did something that will be spread around the school in an hour, and less than likely, what you're being fed inside of the hot lunches (because you never really knew to ask that in primary school).

You'll begin to feel familiar with your daily class schedule and what classes to go to in between breaks. You hear the bell which is the signal for the start of the race to launch. It's comparable to the gun for the horse races and the clamoring feet shuffling between classes. While the stampede is happening, a math lesson happens to fit in by trying to calculate a bathroom break in the midst of all the chaos.

You walk into your classroom; you possibly smell the stale, stuffy air of all the other pupils that had been in the class before you. Walking to your desk setting your backpack or books down, you begin to see all of your other classmates walk into the room and take their seats. In hindsight, it's almost playing out in my head like zombies walking into the classrooms, dark circled eyes, grungy clothes, some sort of foul smell emanating from somewhere, and some who make strange grunting noises. Did I just have a false memory of someone coming toward me asking for brains?

As you and your zombie friends are sitting at your desks, the teacher, the grim reaper of high school, starts discussing your future homework. They, metaphorically, hit you across the face with their yard stick and wake you up from your comfortable zombie-robotic routine of: ringing bell, calculate, shuffle, race, brains, and repeat. You've become comfortable with all of the paperwork you've been given for school and at home, like they are preparing you to work in your cubicle for the rest of your life

Dun Dun Dun! They tell you, brace yourself, you will be giving an oral report. Don't be gross right now, I'm telling you about the horrific public speech! The report you have to give in front of the class. The one where you turn red and feel like everyone is looking at you, because they are! The report that will be talked about you turning red, even though you got a good grade on said report, all because of the public humiliation you had to endure for three to five minutes.

You stand there feeling the beads of sweat forming in your hair, hands, or between your buttcheeks (since you aren't sure if you're going to shit yourself to be more humiliated). You hear the room go quiet. The quiet is either the students being surprised from the sound of a fart, or, the fart that became a wet liquid filling your pants. You can be the judge of whether it's just a shart or that you've full on went "when it comes out your bum like a bullet from a gun...diarrhea diarrhea". They are waiting for your single mess up and then your zombie classmates will rage at you with glaring pointy teeth, their hands outstretched to grab you, and their faces so close like they would do in a Hollywood horror film. Then again, maybe the diarrhea would come in handy to send them off the scent.

Then, you hardly remember about that "trick" of being able to make a public speech by imagining everyone in the room naked. Just so you know, they aren't the naked ones, you are. You're standing up in front of them waiting to be devoured, and you've made it easier for them, because you're freaking naked! You've become the prey and you've given your sacrifice of life on a silver platter for those zombies. You are naked surrounded by predators. You've been tricked by the Grim Reaper Teacher.

This is where the "Naked Years" come into our journey. Standing in front of people during the most awkward time of your life is like sending Mad King

Vulnerability and The Naked Years

Henry to live in a Monastery. Vulnerability is born in a single moment. You are stripped naked, instead of the other way around.

As I've gotten older, the term of being "naked" has completely changed from being a simple speech given in a classroom of students. I imagine each vulnerable moment in a timeline, almost like a belt. A belt that is endless with a smooth front and the back with a few little fuzzy edges, since nothing is perfect. Then I imagine someone taking a small pocket knife. One that is easily flipped out in a moment's notice, in order to gash at it. Once the vulnerable moment comes, it does shape a little bit of how you perceive the moment and how you may change your response for the next similar encounter. The vulnerable moment never goes away though. It stays there, no matter how small or large.

What I imagine is a person, man or woman, in a relationship. In this relationship, you give your all. You give your love, your kindness, your time, and your devotion. You're freely wandering about life and thinking everything is running well through your day to day. Then something happens. It could be as small as finding something suspicious you might brush off at first which then becomes something more significant, or it could be as serious as being assaulted. In this situation, hoping your own mentality is self reliant enough to know you're worth better, you were vulnerable. You had opened up to something and thought it would be okay. You let a piece of yourself out, by feeling safe.

It's okay! You allowed yourself to be naked and vulnerable. You allowed yourself to trust someone you thought cared for you. Just grab your knife and take a stab into that leather belt. This can never be undone. You may be able to patch it a little, but underneath it will always be there. The next time you are in a relationship, there will be a memory of what happened. You may have a bit more hesitancy to be "naked" so soon again, but there will be a learned lesson in it's place. Which, "a lesson learned is a life earned" –Kiyomi's broken brain.

Vulnerability isn't just about a relationship or having a tormented school experience, it was just an easier analogy. Being naked could cause a tear in the leather, but it's something you may be able to mentally repair before making it a trauma. Being naked is also something strong. It may make you a bit more powerful instead of being torn down. You could have the ability to throw your robe off dramatically and say, "I know that I'm not the one, or the only one, at fault for this and I may have put myself out there, but at least I know I was the real one".

Being vulnerable can also be said as, "wearing your heart on your sleeve". To me, the statement is such a load of crap. Being vulnerable means you are in a situation where you can be harmed. Wearing your heart on your sleeve can mean several things. It can be in a positive or negative comment. In a positive way, it could mean you are soft-hearted and care for anyone you become close with, even friends. In a negative way, it could be you are a huge pushover and setting yourself up for vulnerability, which will then turn into a form of harm. Just don't let it get to that point. Row your own boat.

Vulnerability and The Naked Years

From what I've learned about being vulnerable, it's mainly been when I can't control things. I feel stripped down. I feel naked and exposed. I feel like I can't do anything to help myself or to help the situation. I can't help but go back through my mental rewind reel and play back trauma of times where the vulnerability was at its highest, which caused me to have a lot of mental stalls. I don't mean to. It's just like some sort of block where I need to find a solution before I can move forward and know what to do for the next time. It takes a little time and a lot of effort, but I can make a better decision, or know how to react in the future.

In this story, I'm choosing to be vulnerable with you. It's very hard. Harder than it may seem. We may not even know each other in person, which makes me feel a little more naked. I'm pouring many of my thoughts and feelings into something that may not happen or you may not even like. That loss of control is something I'm working through. I want this experience to help make me a better person. I don't know if that's what the end result will be. I think it will make me help myself though. Rather than trying to control it, I'm letting it go. Right here, what you're reading (hopefully), is the release of my nakedness. How do I look? This has become an episode of "Naked and Afraid".

Now, avert your eyes and get out of my tree you "Peeping Tom". Move on to the next chapter.

"Getting over a painful experience is much like crossing monkey bars. You have to let go at some point before you can move forward." –C.S. Lewis

♥Shannon♥

Vulnerability and The Naked Years

This guy. This wonderful man. Shannon and I have known each other for over 10 years. I think it's been around 14 years. We actually met when we started working together. Something clicked with us and I found a kindred spirit in him. Shannon is amazing. He is humble and has the heart of King Midas' gold. Besides Matt, Shannon has been my number one front runner of this entire book. He's given me feedback and has read through chapters like the paper was burning. Shannon is a person, that when he smiles, you know it's completely genuine and you can see the kindness he emanates. You just know, you know? He is one of the good ones. A person that you know would do anything for you just as long as you didn't suffer. Forever and always my kindred spirit.

1. What was your happiest moment as a child? As an adult?

My happiest moments as a child were playing on the beaches of the Oregon Coast near Coos Bay/North Bend where we lived until I was around seven. Spending what seemed like endless days running, or meticulously exploring tide pools and collecting multi colored crabs from beneath saturated rocks on the edges of the pools with my adopted Sister. Racing out into the sea and letting the waves carry me back in safely to the shore, saltwater stinging my nose the whole way. Climbing on the huge rocks of the jetties while my Dad fished until I had no more energy and fell fast asleep on the flat stony surfaces. The repetitive crashing, but calming sounds of the ocean's waves lulling me into deep dreams. Often, my Dad would scoop me up in the evenings and carry me home to bed.

My happiest moments as an adult have been, hands down, every single moment and memory from when I was able to be a Step-Up Daddy to a certain little girl named Gracen for 3.5 years. While her Mother and I were together she gave new purpose to my existence. I adored being a Dad and excelled at it. I cannot have children of my own due to medical reasons, so when I say the experience was an ineffable blessing to me, I mean it with all my heart. I wouldn't trade those memories for anything and i am looking hopefully forward to the day I may resume my role in her life. As relationships sometimes do,the one between her Mother and I became damaged..So I must wait for time to heal it with all patience.

2. What's the most beautiful thing you've ever witnessed? What's the most beautiful thing you can give to someone else?

The most beautiful thing I've ever witnessed was when I first began working as a caregiver in an adult family home for elderly women with dementia. Two of the women in their late nineties were sitting together at the dining table having soup for lunch. One of them was feeling poorly that day, and had been very vocal about it because she felt so miserable. She wasn't eating. The woman to her immediate left at the table was an old Scottish gal whom everyone loved dearly. All the doctors on both women's care teams had long since stated that all understanding of their surroundings as well as any personality traits such as empathy had long since been claimed by their disease processes. however all f us in the room were taken by surprise to look over and see the Scottish woman's outstretched arm, with steaming soup laden spoon in hand, reaching over to comfort her suffering friend. Smiling ear to ear as she did and saying "You've got to eat, Dearie!" That's always stuck with me. It's been eighteen years now I've been in the industry of healthcare and still that resonates. Our humanity, our capacity to care for others is stronger than even the most thieving of diseases...

The most beautiful thing I believe I can give anyone is my heart.

3. What makes you feel wealthy in life or love? What could you add to your life that would make you feel wealthier than you already are?

The only thing that's ever made me feel wealthy in life is family. Being around the ones i love and seeing the smiles and listening to the interactions. Telling a joke and having everyone around me in the family laugh and knowing somehow all that laughter was present in the world right then because I was there in that moment. Holding my Daughter while I could and listening to her sing and laugh because she felt safe and secure to do so in my arms. Having that responsibility and feeling so blessed to have had it bestowed upon me. Picking a corner at Christmas and just observing everyone I love in a giant circle existing, breathing, being happy and feeling at home together. That's wealthy to me. That's what it's all about...

♥ 10 ♥

Future

I'm sitting here, in complete darkness other than the dimmed light from my laptop, again. I've found I write when I'm inspired, it comes from my heart and gut, rather than my head. Without going back through the chapters, and solely focusing on what I remember, I think we talked about how I had made a list of points I want to converse with you. This one, tonight, was not one I thought we would discuss until later. However, tonight, I'm not even going to pretend this isn't crossing my mind and keeping me awake at 12:45 AM.

Minutes ago, my four year old daughter was crying and yelling from her bedroom. She was sitting on her bed with only the small Christmas lights, we've yet to take down, lighting the room. Her words were jumbled and I couldn't quite make sense of what she was actually saying. Her little hands were folded beneath her with her legs criss-crossed. We believe she has some sleep walking issues, since one evening she told me she was in a cup and couldn't get out, while walking toward my bed.

Before, and I mean not far long ago, being honest here, I would get so upset when my children wouldn't let me sleep through the night. I'd felt like I'd been robbed some nights where all I wanted was just one uninterrupted night's sleep. My kids are night owls, even on a routine, it's just their natural functional state. So every night, and I mean every night, I'd be woken up to crying and wailing from my daughter, or my son telling me he had a nice nap at 3 a.m.. I'd get frustrated and felt like ripping out my hair while I clenched my jaw and my eyes bulged out. It didn't matter what time it was, it was just always an inconvenience to me, and my lack of sleep. All I thought about was how much pain I would be in the next morning. My head would throb with each heart beat and would burn like acid was being poured down my spine. I'd have to ice it all day long and wonder how I would make it through. I can't have caffeine so, quite honestly, I'm not sure how I do make it through.

A few nights ago, my daughter did her normal late night wakeup. She'd not come into my room this time and did the wailing in her room, on her bed, instead. I peeked around the door and the sweet little curly haired girl was in a ball shape, crying. I looked at her sympathetically. My baby. My sweet girl was in a place of mind I couldn't see. I felt like I couldn't do anything to make her remember where she was. I walked slowly to her and tried to talk calmly and quietly. I whispered things to help her remember where she was and who loved her. She just kept crying. I tried rubbing her back and singing a soft song to her. Still she kept crying like she was hurt somehow. There was nothing I could do, except be there for her. No amount of words, songs, or back rubs, would do anything as much as just being there for my girl. So, I lifted her up and she instantly moved her arms outstretched like she knew she was going to be held, and I cradled her. It reminded me of that book "I'll love you forever", where the mother sneaks into her child's room and holds him and rocks him because she knows she won't be able to do it forever. She takes every opportunity she can to absorb every moment of her sweet boy and at the end, the son holds his mother and it's implied that she's dying. He then returns home to his own child and rocks her the way his mother did for him.

I remembered when babies are born, they thrive on the skin to skin contact. My daughter was always attached to me. She never wanted anyone else. Just me. So in this moment where there was nothing I could do, where I was helpless to my own tiny life I'd created, I cradled her. I was wearing a low cut tank top and I made sure her ear was against my chest so she could hear my heart beating. So she could listen to the steady breathing, I purposefully filled my lungs with, even though I just wanted to cry. I thought her listening to my breathing and my heart beating would help her steady, which would put her in a calmer state.

She instantly stopped crying. She was still slightly awake, or in some sort of state where she felt she could move to get comfortable as I held her in my right arm. She wrapped her left arm under my right arm and around the right side of my waist. She then lifted her right arm and sent her hand flying directly up toward the left of my neck. This position was almost exactly how I remembered breast feeding her. The instant thought of her calming, just from being in my arms and being against my skin, made my heart swell with regret. All this time I couldn't help but be angry when I was so sleep deprived. Here was my sweet girl who just needed me. She needed me. She needed her mom.

In that moment, I knew any other time I heard her fearful cry, I would go into her room, lift her into my lap and hold her like I did that night. I would make time for her in my arms, for her to feel safe, and for me to be a loving and devoted mother, to a child who needed love in the middle of the night. I rocked her as that mother did in the book for her son.

As I sat in her bed just moments ago, I held her like I did and like I promised that I'd do. I cried as I looked down at her, sleeping and feeling calm. I saw the way her eyelashes fanned out across her cheek. I saw the little cupids bow on her top lip and how the bottom lip was a full pouty one like mine. I held her head in my arms and heard her breaths with each sigh against my chest. I tried so hard to keep my breaths steady, as tears streamed down my face. I could feel her hair gaining an imprint of wetness, from my face pressed against her head, while my tears seeped out. So many other revelations became clear to me that hadn't before. All I could think about was how much I wanted this moment to last forever. As I sat there rocking her gently, I gazed up toward the ceiling corner. I noted all of the colored Christmas lights, just to keep that entire moment repeating in my head. I noted the feeling of sitting on her memory foam mattress and how I slightly sank to fit into it. If I can't remember that moment again, I want to know that I had it, and it did happen. I want to remember how it wouldn't last forever, no matter how painful. My children will grow up and I won't be able to hold them the way I used to and be there for them the way they needed me when small. Then the reality hit me even harder.

My daughter is the age when my family moved out of the house where my biological father had relapsed using heroin. My son is the age of when my father passed away. I thought of how disheartening it would be for them to grow up the way I did. I can barely remember my dad. I started wondering if it would be the same for them. Would they have to rely on the memories of others to have any type of memory of me? That robbed feeling of knowing that that person was there, but not having the memories to support the fact.

With everything happening so quickly with all of the medical juggling, I forgot to look at everything around me in fine detail. The way my daughter's face looks when she randomly says she loves me or the way my son shakes his butt and they both laugh so hard. I forgot to look at how the future of our family would look like, without taking those fine details.

Our future as a family, your future with your family, is not laid out in every scene before you. We go about our day to days. Sometimes, not thinking twice about the single second after, what could happen. We don't think of making sure to take the extra time the night before. We don't think to imprint every single moment of ourselves into the people who love us most. They will go over every detail they can of us, if we were not to come home later. They will recall the memory of how they saw you last and what you talked about together. They might have regret or a feeling of "I wish". The opposite, as us being the one who is leaving, we don't think about walking out the door and into our car. We don't know that that would be the day we'd take our last breath.

The world right now is so fast, it's so focused on money and how quickly someone can have it ready for you. We forget that our future is in our family. Our children, our family related to us if we don't have children, our dearest friends, they are all our future. Their memory will be what is left to tell stories about us. Our future is in another human, as memories. We are but a fragment of the world. We are a memory right now. Our past is what shapes how the memories of us will continue, but our future is but only just a thought. Grasping that is near impossible. We can plan for a future. We can hope for a future. It's the matter of that thought of the future truly becoming our reality. If your loved ones spoke of you, how would you want to be remembered?

Looking at my children tonight and feeling a heart ache like nothing I've experienced, has opened my eyes to a hope of my future. February 8th has changed me so much. I've pondered things before, especially after the brain surgery. I was sure my life would be back to normal. I'd be living life to the fullest with my family and being thankful for the days I had spending with them. My friend told me that everyone thought the same; I would be back to my old self and remembering the broken fragment of time where we went through a troubled storm.

Tonight, now at 1:32 AM, I'm sitting in the dark, still apart from my dim light computer screen. I'm quietly crying by myself in the way where you don't want to wake someone up, sobbing and scolding myself for not being in my moments in order to make my future. Tears are streaming down my face while I stare into a trance from sobbing, typing, but almost not able to make out the words. How dare I take advantage of my future? How dare I forget every moment I make with someone else is a memory for both of us? They will remember whatever they can about me. With my friends included in this book, I'm trying to make a memory about them.

We are selfish beings. While our past can't change, it does shape our future. Each and every one of us. We forget life is but a dream. We move on about our days, forgetting that we become the dream for others when we are gone. I can't change how I've felt or what I've done, but I know what I can do from now on. I can do better, or at least, make the best effort I can.

I could say, "Back to the Future" for our end of this chapter. However, even the statement going back into our future, is still saying it's gone.

So, instead I'll say, "Keep the past and move to the future".

❤11❤

Settle

Never settle.
　Period.
　If we go through life thinking this is the best that we can do, how are we supposed to grow? That question was metaphorical and mental. The mental part of it can drive you crazy or help you get a grip on your life and change some things you know you can change.
　Please don't get me wrong. Settling and being happy are two very different things for me. To me, settling is coming to a compromise of your life that makes you just accept things the way they are. Being happy is making changes needed in order to not settle and to know that you did everything you needed to making it the best you absolutely could.
　Since you already know I had the tumor resected and have a plate in my head, you also remember that between surgery, September 4th, 2015, and March of

2017, I was having "episodes" we now know are seizures. We won't focus too much on that again since we've already discussed it. However, I went nearly two years of undiagnosed seizures along with countless medications. One of the countless "helpful" specialists, tried to tell me that the medications weren't working because I didn't have a positive enough attitude. BITCH, I WILL TAKE YOU DOWN! Needless to say, I broke up with her.

I bring up those topics because during those times of trial, giving up was never an option. It was definitely in a vision at times, but I knew I never would give up. Therefore, it was never an option. There were countless doctors, specialists, prescriptions, and natural remedies I tried that never gave any headway or relief. I tried everything someone threw at me. What did I have to lose?

"In the confrontation between the stream and the rock, the stream always wins- not through strength but by perseverance." –H. Jackson Brown

My husband and I loved to take drives through the back roads. It was something we did when we were newly together and it's been something we've loved to do with our kids. Sometimes we would be arguing and we knew it was time to just pick up the keys and get in the car. When you're in a car and arguing, you'll either both die from crashing from anger, or you'll get to a point where you can speak to each other without being able to storm off, since you're stuck in a confined space. It's a point where communication is formed, even if it's uncomfortable for a while.

There's something about hearing the steady of the pavement under the tires. There's a feeling of comfort when slowly swaying around each turn or corner. My favorite was when it would be summer, we would have the windows down and the air would be much cooler from the scorch of the day. The air smelled a bit humid and sweet. It was a much sweeter smell than fall or winter.

After the episodes became a regular routine, going on a drive became near impossible. If I was in a car or even on a treadmill for a small amount of time, I would fall prey that night. I'd begin having symptoms in the late afternoon. It would start as a sick feeling coming over me and I'd feel out of body. We would start preparing for nightfall and by that time, I'd be completely bed ridden. I would go through waves of focusing on breath going in and breath going out, just so I knew I still was breathing. I would feel an uncomfortable tingling on the left side of my body. There was also a heaviness that was similar to a tickle. It reminded me of when a part of your body falls asleep but it is a heaviness instead of those pins and needles feeling. As you would shake out the dead heaviness, it would feel similar to a heavy tickle. I would lie on the bed and feel the heaviness build and fill my body, visually comparable to water immediately filling a glass from the tap. As I focused on my breaths, the release of the heaviness played out in electrical volts and jolts fleeing from my left arm and leg. Hours on end, I'd be trapped in this cycle.

This cycle is what finally produced help. It's when I became medicated on a daily basis so I could function through the day. It was when someone finally took notice. The reason it came to some form of a result, was having the "episodes" every day. They were intense. I would even start to fear them because I knew exactly what would happen. It's when the diagnosis of seizures was put into my charts and was finally read in a more serious manner.

I can't explain the anger I felt from every ounce about all of it. The anger inside of me wanted to call all of the other specialists, doctors, and nay-sayers just to tell them to shove it. I KNEW there was something wrong and they missed it. They missed it every time and told me it was in my head. However, it doesn't matter how much I would say to them, it doesn't matter how angry I've been, and it doesn't matter how much pain I'm in, even though it's horrible. What matters, I, Me, Myself, didn't give up. I never settled for what someone else told me. I never let them tell me what I felt or what I knew was right, deep down to my core, was wrong.

I've had two incredible doctors. One was my general practitioner. I won't mention her name, but it was so important to me to include her in this conversation.

I found her while searching for a new GP since I was getting nowhere. I saw her picture and I knew right then, I knew she would be the one to understand. I don't know how, but I just did. Again, one of my "gut" instincts.

I called their office and luckily, she was accepting new patients. When I met her for the first time, her face was beaming. Her persona was captivating. She had short blonde hair that barely reached her chin and a genuine smile that reached her eyes. She was tall, but not so much that I felt too small. This woman wasn't overpowering, but she was definitely someone you would remember and think of the strength and confidence upon meeting her. When I think back now of her walking into the clinical office room upon the first time of meeting her, I swear I can envision a halo rotating above her head. I can see a golden light streaming from the halo, at the base very bright and vibrant. Then it would flow into an ombre below, just above her golden hair, perfect for the entire analogy. This reminded me of how the colors of a fresh rainbow would blend seamlessly together.

After that official first office visit, I would diligently come into her office and have follow up visits. She would look at my complex case in sincerity at every appointment. She had typing fingers that would flood the keyboard. She would tell me about different things she wanted to try or just to rule out, at that point. It wasn't a complete let down when tests would come back negative, because it still narrowed down the endless list. At every appointment, hearing about test results not confirming anything, I would tell her I just must be crazy. Still, at every single appointment, she would tell me I wasn't.

"You're not crazy. I can tell you, you're not crazy. We WILL figure this out, and some of this will change. I've said this to another woman, and guess what? We figured it out and she's living a different life now", is what that angel of a doctor, told me. She was incredible and wonderful amidst everything she was going through in her own life. You know who you are, if you're reading this. I just want to say an undying and immense, "Thank you". It might not be everything we thought of, but you were the one. The only one to believe me and the first to see what was happening. The only one who was able to bring me to a point of living ANY type of life, which was better than the one I had been currently living.

The other life changer is actually my current specialist. The very first time my husband and I met her was when I had to have a video EEG done. It feels like they scrub your scalp with a brillo pad, stick frequency electrodes on those abrasions left behind of the scalp you once had, then come out looking like some sort of mutated octopus. It feels like tentacles have burst out of your head but instead of eight tentacles, there are millions. Of course this is an exaggeration. I think there's only One million. On top of it, you're attached to a pack that resembles a fanny pack, and the attachments are all of your tentacles bundled together under a cloth to make it look like you have an umbilical cord coming from the back of your head. To sum it up, you're ridiculous looking.

The video EEG is completely uncomfortable. Hospital beds are never an easy adjustment, especially when trying to maneuver around the IV leeched onto your body. They have you stay in the hospital bed and they watch you from a video camera. The most uncomfortable experience is having to be off of all seizure medications. They have to be able to record seizure activity, and the seizures are obviously controlled with medication. Once they are able to get a few seizures recorded, the doctor comes in to tell you what they've seen or didn't see. They then remove your tentacles to release you from tentacle jail and you go home.

A few days of being trapped and my husband sleeping on the steel chair bed that is so graciously complimentary, the time had come for her to tell me if I was having real seizures or the pseudoseizures. Pseudoseizures are episodes that resemble seizures but are on a psychological level that can result from an emotional origin. I truly thought because of all of the stress I've gone through, I was having pseudoseizures and that I would be sent home and all would be right in the world again by just having some extra emotional support from a therapist. However, she told me she thought the seizures were coming from a deep part of my brain.

After all of that time wondering, anger coursing through my veins, and after so many tears, this woman just handed me something that had taken her only four days to analyze. In four days, when every other specialist over two years said no, she was able to report to me she believed I was having seizures deep within my brain and it would take much more time to work things out for the best outcome. I had chills run through my body producing visible goose bumps. I started to cry and nearly shake.

In a way, I wish it would have been pseudoseizures. However, because of the diagnosis, she did give me an enormous amount of relief. After those 18 months of myself and husband telling everyone that there was something wrong, then having them all respond it was me, she gave me relief it wasn't all in my head. I hadn't gone through all of that turmoil just for another person to tell me I was wrong, yet again. I sat there in shock as she held the plastic brain that came apart for educational purposes. She showed Matt and me where she thought the seizures were originating. To be honest, I remember very little about any of it. Thankfully she printed out a paper explaining everything, which I was able to read later.

I didn't settle. I did not settle for what the rest of them all told me was wrong. The pain I felt was real, the episodes were real.

"Curiosity killed the cat but satisfaction brought it back." There is no such thing as too many questions.

I've heard that saying, "Are you an idiot just because someone tells you, you are?". I had never processed that saying until now, even upon hearing it. If you know your body and feel something is truly wrong, do not settle for just one person to tell you it's just you. If someone tells you there is a certain way how you should feel, cover your ears, quick! They are trying to make you feel lower than them, even if they don't realize it. Just like if someone says that you aren't exceptional or amazing, it's a big, fat, lie. In those moments, they are putting themselves in a higher regard. I'll raise my hand on when I mentally called one of the doctors a bitch. Mainly because I was angry at her and I still am. I still am not in higher regard than her. Likely, I just stooped down to her level. Thankfully I didn't call her one out loud.

Don't settle. Please don't. Don't tell yourself you are okay with being in a spot where you don't feel is your fullest potential. You, yes you, are worthy of a wonderful life. You are worthy of forgiveness and kindness. Just because someone tells you something negative about yourself, does not mean you are. Do not settle for what someone else thinks of you. If they call you a name, just ask yourself if you think it's true. If your answer is no, then it doesn't matter and it's not worth your time fighting about it. Go on about your day and fill your life with people who support you and who tell you positive things to uplift you. Go row your freaking boat away from them. They are the clown, on the shore, trying to drown you.

If you do something idiotic, or hurt someone, apologize and move on. It doesn't matter if they get over it or not. Their harbor of their emotions is not your problem. However, saying "Sorry" means you'll NEVER do it again. So, being sincere is the focus.

Be kind, be humble, be the best version of you. Don't settle for a life that's not what you have dreamed about. Don't allow someone else to fill your head with nonsense about you. You know you, better than anyone. Strive to be happy.

"Things are the way they are. We suffer because we imagine different." –Rachel Wolchin.

Alicia

HeARTwork

I don't know how long I've known Alicia. A lot of it is due to my memory of upon actually knowing her but also because I don't remember a lot of middle school or high school anymore. I do know that we've known each other at least 20 years. When you grow up in a small town like ours, you usually know everyone from kindergarten. We were able to reconnect and she is a beacon of light. She would give you anything she has to help you. She would actually, literally, be a person who would give you the shirt off of her back if she knew you needed it. She's become a Naturopathic Doctor and it has changed so much of how she views, and the rest of us who get to be educated, the earth and the universe. She's an amazing conversation starter and will have your stomach with six pack abs from an afternoon chat/laugh session. I'm very lucky to have her in this life and grateful we get to walk this earth together. She is definitely someone who is making such an incredible impact on this world.

1. What was your happiest moment as a child? As an adult?

As a child I was happiest when I spent time with my family. We often spent summers with my cousins, aunt and uncles and grandparents at the coast or the mountains. We are a very close family and we always have an incredible time when we gather. My happiest moment as an adult was celebrating earning my doctorate degree with my family and friends at my home. The sun was out, the flowers were gorgeous and all my family and friends showed up to party with me, it was wonderful.

2. What's the most beautiful thing you've ever witnessed? What is the most beautiful thing you could give to someone else?

The most beautiful thing I have ever witnessed was my Dad's family coming together through the passing of my grandma. She knew she had come to the end of her battle with her health conditions and my family all came together and supported her through the very end. The most beautiful thing I could give to someone else is the power to see the true beauty inside themself and find the gifts they have to share with the world.

3. What makes you feel wealthy in life or love? What could you add to your life that would make you more wealthy than you already are?

I feel wealthy when I see feel true joy in others and myself. Seeing my nieces giggle and smile or my dogs waiting excitedly to chase their orange ball through the field. I am always looking to add more wonderful people and life experiences into my life. And the more incredibly unique people I meet and experiences I have enrich my life in innumerable ways.

♥ 12 ♥

Forgive don't Forget

Remember I told you there has been a lot of grief? In grief, things can sometimes be unresolved. Especially if someone you've known or cared about suddenly dies. So many things were left unsaid and there may have been so much forgiveness needed. Regret could even flood the mind. Those are all devastating. It's so much turmoil I think everyone forgets about forgiving. Forgiving yourself and forgiving someone else are still the same act. It may be a different process in certain ways, but forgiveness is forgiveness.

To forgive someone is not for their benefit, no matter how much someone tries to turn it. To forgive someone actually relieves you from the mountain of negative emotions that create an echo inside.

"I can't afford to hate people. I don't have that kind of time." –Bob Ross

Forgive don't Forget

I've been guilty grasping onto what I shouldn't, on so many levels. As have we all at times, I'm sure. I'm still trying to learn, honestly. Maybe writing this out will help me release just one of the things I need to forgive. Forgiving someone, especially if they've wronged you, is so difficult especially if they aren't apologetic or verbalize an apology. Forgiving them just means that your mind releases the anger or whatever emotion that's eating you alive. My mom always says, "Don't let someone live rent free in your head".

Clinging to negative emotions causes stress, and it's already been proven that stress has a huge impact on your wellbeing, as well as your life span. Sometimes just speaking out the negative feeling toward something or someone helps to start the forgiving process.

Now comes something probably not often heard. Forgive, but don't forget. Most people have heard, "Forgive and forget", you mustn't forget. I'll explain why.

Forget, defined, means "Fail to remember". I'm writing this book to remember. Why would anyone want to forget? To forget would mean any type of lesson you've learned from that experience, could be repeated.

A family member of ours is heavily into the drug scene. At one point in time, she had taken money out of my wallet to use for her addiction. Since then, she's been continuously arrested and in and out of jail. The thing is, whenever she is incarcerated, I try to write her a letter for her to know I love her. I do love her. I miss who she was when she wasn't using. I forgive her, but I don't forget the stealing. I won't forget because that has taught me to not keep my personal things out and about for everyone to see or take advantage of the situation. This is where that saying, "Love them from a distance" can come up. I can love her and cherish the great memories we have together, but know at this point in time, I can't trust her. That's alright. I'd rather have to love someone from a distance than to be an enabler.

Becoming an enabler is a fraction of my own definition of "Forgive and Forget". In that instance, you forgive the action and the person, which is great, but then you forget. So what happens for the next time? For me and for my own memories, forgive but don't forget.

This concept can be used for any of type of situation. A former relationship, something could have ended nasty or in a way that you felt was unfit from the counterpart. You can forgive them but not forget. You free your mind of being held by whatever has held you back, but you don't forget so that you can base another relationship on, for you, what you do want and what's just unacceptable.

What I need to come face to face with is the forgiveness toward everyone who told me I was wrong. The ones who told me that when I wasn't well, that I could have been dramatizing it or that it just couldn't possibly be, are the ones that I need to forgive. No emotion or thought is going to change any outcome that has happened since the surgery. Right now, I need to focus on the memory making and the time that I do have to be with the ones I love and trust.

This isn't a long chapter, mainly because it's simple. The words and thoughts are there. Most of the time, forgiveness' journey takes quite a long time to even start forward. Sometimes forgiveness is just a thought that people have but feel like they can't find it.

I don't want to get into a lot of religion in this book. I believe that's something private, of my own, of your own, and just plain "friend sabotaging" to bring up at parties. However, I want to discuss the Amish. The reason, I believe we all have it backward and the Amish have it right in front of them.

My mom had made a valid point one day about forgiveness that profoundly resonated in my head and in my heart. This isn't word for word, but what she had mentioned was that we should be more like the Amish. I mean, we could learn a lot from them aside from the forgiveness aspect, since they most likely will be the ones to survive any type of apocalypse. Though, she was speaking about their way of forgiveness. She had mentioned the Amish forgive at the very first moment they need to.

I'm not sure if anyone remembers the Amish school shooting. I truly just can't stomach going into the gruesome details. To sadly sum it up, a man went into an Amish schoolhouse and opened fire among Amish children. However, the Amish family and community had forgiven the man that executed their children and himself, nearly immediately. The media had begun focusing on their points of forgiveness and reconciliation. I bring this up because the Amish invert the process of forgiveness. This doesn't mean they would have run up to the gunman and started hugging him, had he lived. Their process of forgiveness is it does not hoist a piano laced with revenge over someone's head. They would have seen justice presented upon him, not out for revenge, but for punishment for his actions. The way that the Amish forgive is comparable to Jesus' love; it's how they believe forgiveness to be. It's love. They offered words of encouragement to the man's mother, wife, other family, and had brought food and hugs with them. The Amish even attended the funeral of the gunman even though some had just buried their own children. The wife of the shooter was invited to the intimate funerals of the victims. She inevitably wrote a letter to them regarding their kindness and love. It had been something that not only helped her family for a forgiveness they felt they so desperately needed, but it changed their community. It blew me away the thought of love through such a trial. What a beautifully heartbreaking ordeal.

The Amish forgive so they will be forgiven in return, since we are all still selfish beings. None of us are free of sin or deceit. They hope to live in the type of love they would have seen from Jesus. No matter what religion you are, living in love seems so much more powerful than living in anger and hate. They forgive willfully in their religion because no amount of anger, remorse, tragedy, or revenge will rewind the time to relive what has happened. Clutching and drooling onto the thought of revenge is consuming regret and anger like it's chocolate during PMS.

This is already starting to sink into my forgetful brain. I hope I can take this information and retain it. I want to live peacefully and hopefully have a mindset that goes into the rest of this life, with grace. Most of all, love.

Forgive don't Forget

Live in love, for however long your journey, and forgive but don't forget.

♥13♥

While we're here...Kindness

With forgiveness, I feel like kindness comes hand in hand.

I imagine Kindness as tall, dark, and handsome. A peaceful look swept across his face, slow-motion walking while wearing a breezy, white button down shirt, as his hair wisps in the golden wind. He's of course on a paradise beach and all of a sudden, still in slow-motion, he sees the profile of Forgiveness. She's standing at a profile view, alone on the beach, looking out into the sea with her feet slightly in the water. The wind is blowing her beautiful long, perfectly wavy hair, backward, along with the long white, sheer, sheet of a dress. The waves splash slightly up to her ankles, each time the tide of waves comes in.

She glances, in slow motion, at Kindness. It's love at first sight. They slow motion run to each other. With love, forgiveness, and kindness brewing about, Mother Teresa was born.

All jokes aside, because Mother Teresa was a truly wonderful person, forgiveness is what will heal you, but kindness is what will keep the loving people around you. Have you heard of the term "Pay it forward"? It's a way to do a kindness to someone in hopes that they will do something kind for someone else.

I am coming out of my shell again and going to tell you a secret I've been keeping. There are very few people that know about this, and it's usually because they are in the car with me while I do it. Don't get gross; I do so many other things in my car. What I choose to do occasionally (maybe every time), I pay for a person in line behind me or sometimes two and three people behind me, what they were going to order. Most of the time, I don't let them see my face. I do a lot of them at a Starbucks drive thru. I don't look at their faces, I don't wait to see their reactions and I hurry enough so they can't remember my car. If no one is in line behind me, I ask if there is anyone at the counter. If there is no one there, I buy a gift card and ask they use it each time a customer comes through until the card is empty.

I've done nice things for people before, and I like to think of myself as a nice person. I also think when you give kindness, it's on purpose and mindful. There is a difference between being polite and being kind. I'm telling you this, coming clean about my secret, because that purposeful act of kindness could be the difference between seeing something good in a day, or being pessimistic through the rest of it.

I thought about the many times Matt and I would be in the car driving back and forth from Seattle. We would be driving and dreading whatever news we would get, or lack of news. Once the dreaded appointment was over, we would drive home mentally, emotionally, and physically tired after hearing I was crazy or we needed more tests done. Either direction it went, it felt like some sort of dead end. Still, we would have our kids to come home to, so we would get a break and be able to forget the dark cloud looming for a little while.

Most of those days driving, we would stop at Starbucks, coffee shop, or for lunch. The Seattle trips were the reason I decided that I would offer lunch or a coffee to be an act of kindness. I absolutely dreaded the Seattle trips and hearing about tumors, craniotomies, outcomes, yada-yada-yada. I thought that an act of kindness for someone else, maybe having a moment of feeling low or having to contemplate something enormous, maybe even having to hear bad news, would have just that tiny bit of kindness or goodness in their day. When I give the barista the money to pay for however many people I can for that day, I pass along a message for them to say to my unsuspecting victims, "Tell them to have a wonderful day, don't worry about the small things, and remember happiness can be anywhere".

You don't have to flush your bank account to be kind on purpose. Being kind is anything you feel you go beyond what you would normally do. You don't even have to go out of your way to be kind to strangers, either. If you have a loved one, think of what they cherish or what reminds them of something they love. Do a drawing, find it on the earth, or buy it in the shop they saw it. It truly doesn't matter what or how you do it. My grandmother loved butterflies. I remember the flowers I saw in her garden when I was a child. If I could, I would have loved to have drawn a picture of a butterfly on one piece of a paper, then on the other, had a pressed flower. The thought and going out of your way to do it, is kindness. You should still be polite, because it's good manners. Using kindness is so much more than polite. It's giving a piece of you and a piece of your time to someone else.

Think of something someone has mindfully done for you. Now, imagine the feeling you got when it happened.

Please have compassion. Please be generous, friendly and considerate. Please go about life with a little bit more kindness added. To forgive is to allow forgiveness to come to you. To give kindness is to allow kindness to come to you.

Think of Kindness and Forgiveness' beach, while they run side by side. They end up married and having a baby, named Love.

Go buy them a wedding gift, post haste!

♥Kaaren♥

While we're here...Kindness

O h my. I've known Kaaren about the same time frame as Alicia and Kateland. Most memories from middle school and high school are with Kaaren. She is another person whose family has become another family to me. My brother even lived at her house for a short time. Kaaren and I would laugh and stay up all night from a sleepover. We watched movies and ate popcorn like it was the last bag on earth. We came up with silly words that we would be able to tell each other and no one else would know about. SHIBBY! (Sorry, that's a secret between us, not just me!) I was able to be a lot more of myself with her. I think she knew early on about my "gift". It may be why our friendship was so easy and I didn't feel like I needed to hide anything. Anytime I see anything Harry Potter related, Kaaren is the first person I think of. I love her so much. Yes, she is the Harry Potter glasses girl.

1. What was your happiest moment as a child? As an adult?

When I was 10 my mother bought season tickets to The 5th Ave Theater in Seattle. Every couple months my mother and I would take the day and go to Seattle together, just her and I. We would watch a professional musical and go out for a meal together and I had her undivided attention. We would talk about the play we had seen, our dreams and goals, and many other aspects of life. We had season tickets for many years and saw hundreds of musicals together. I cherish these memories and think about how happy I was to be with my mother doing something we both loved!

The happiest I have ever been as a adult was at Disneyland with my daughter. She was six weeks old and I wore her in a baby carrier while on rides and walking around the park. When she was hungry we went to the baby center and I nursed her in their nursing room, then we would go back out for more adventures. To be able to be in one of my favorite places with my child was such an amazing feeling. I know she won't remember the trip but I know that the energy and happiness I was giving off was a powerful bonding experience for us

2. What's the most beautiful thing you've ever witnessed? What is the most beautiful thing you could give to someone else?

Watching my new born child be soothed just by the familiarity of her fathers voice mere minutes after birth is the most beautiful thing I have ever seen. He talked to her in my belly often and read stories to her so she knew his voice well by the time she was born. While I was passing the afterbirth and being stitched up post birth my husband accompanied her to the new born panda bed where they took her blood sugar, weight, etc. She was poked and prodded but didn't make a sound. Dan spoke in low tones to her about how perfect she was and how happy he was to meet her and she stared up at him in awe. Their unbroken eye contact and the love in my husband's eyes was breathtaking.

3. What makes you feel wealthy in life or love? What could you add to your life that would make you wealthier than you already are?

I am wealthy in my family. We are so lucky to be able to live in a multi-generational household where we get along and enjoy each other's company. My daughter (and soon my unborn son) will be able to share a special bond with their grandmas because they will see them every day. I have always been blessed to have a mother who loves me unconditionally and wanted to be my mother desperately. She was very intentional as a mother and cherished every moment we have together (and still does). I can talk to my mother about anything and we are best friends. I continue to be blessed because she married a woman who has a childlike soul and loves that she has found a new family. Despite never having children of her own she has taken to being a mother naturally and is a wonderful grandmother. My husband's mother gets along with my parents and will soon be living with us as well. She has a wealth of knowledge about childcare and babies as she has been a RN specializing in mother baby care and babies with special medical needs. She is invaluable to have near when you have an infant in the house and she is the reason why I was successful at breastfeeding my daughter. I feel wealthy that I can help our parents age in place and stay with their family where they can get the best care for them. The only thing I can add to my life to make me wealthier is already on the way. Our healthy baby boy will be joining us and then my life will be overflowing with wealth and happiness!

♥14♥

Love

The baby of forgiveness and kindness is love. It's the most beautiful baby you've ever seen. However, to get to the point of love, you get a little scraped up. It's only natural.

"Love conquers all", is the quote that has become so famous. I actually never knew who wrote it, until I just looked it up. It's actually not the complete quote. It's, "Love conquers all things; let us too surrender to Love". It was said by a Roman poet named Virgil, or otherwise known, Vergilius Maro.

First, let's focus on the first quote, the one where it says "Love conquers all". When I first read that, I shook my head and laughed. I don't know if it was because I was too young and stupid to know what it truly meant, but I laughed. I thought there was no way that love can conquer all. The example I kept playing out in my mind was actually about relationships. How would love conquer all in an abusive relationship, or something that was done to have left a scar emotionally or physically? I truly just scoffed at the notion.

At one point, during marriage especially, I constantly thought that when they would say, "Love conquers all" I felt like saying, "Sometimes love isn't enough" or more point blank, "Shut up you wanker". Naively, I felt like I knew that was true. Love just wasn't enough. It wasn't enough for me to forgive or forget things, which we all know the conclusion that I came to. It wasn't enough for me to say I would be willing to accept things that were tragic and say because of love, it would make it all better.

I was looking at things all wrong. I was looking at everything backward. I was looking at it from the point of love would heal everything that was broken and continued to be shattered. I was trying to make it about how things in the world could never be the same and no matter what, love would never change that.

"Love conquers all" doesn't mean love covers things completely like they've never happened. It means love can rise above anything in life we go through and helps to heal what love we've seemed to have lost, especially our self-love. I see now why it says how it conquers all. Yes, of course there was something terrible that happened. Acknowledge it. Love will still be there to help, even when you don't think anything good can come out of a situation.

A tragedy occurs, maybe a natural disaster, and it leaves a mess of things. It leaves a mess emotionally, physically, mentally, it's just there. No matter what it is, there will be a love that comes out of the woodwork with no expectation. Maybe a home was destroyed in a fire; the whole community comes together to help the family with food or shelter. That's love. The love that surrounds us in a way that we don't expect is what conquers all. Love is what shelters us from the "all" that we will experience. Everyone in life will experience that "all". It doesn't exclude anyone.

After reading the rest of the quote, "Love conquers all things; let us too surrender to Love", it makes much more sense. Love shelters us and we must be able to surrender to it in order to experience it.

Imagine the tragedy of someone losing their home. There was a fire and the family lost nearly or all of their belongings. Their neighbors see them standing in the road covered in black ash. The family stares at the flames being extinguished, while their minds spin about what items were close to their heart being destroyed in engulfing flames and being helpless to it.

Once the fire is put to rest, but the sadness grows by the second, the community comes together to offer their help with whatever they can. They offer their love. The family's surrender to love is about acceptance. It isn't about selfishness or being superior to not want the help. It's about accepting the love that others give you and accept that in the face of whatever "all" you experience, someone is there for you.

So, now I'm older and wiser (sometimes), I can fully understand what it means. It's something I want to remember, specifically about love. Love can envelope you and help you, as long as you allow love to be in your life. I really appreciate understanding that now. I don't want to forget love conquers all.

What my momma has said about love is it can be fierce. It can be fiercely fighting with your every being, especially when you know lives are in danger. I experienced fierce love when I had my children. It became a moment when you love something so deeply you don't even think about yourself. I've seen people become so angry at their child being hurt. I would be so angry and irrational. I know I would be. I know the fierce nature of our instincts would immediately take over and it wouldn't matter the aftermath. It would be about the then and now.

I just watched a very sad interview about a man whose daughter was sexually abused. He had to hear the testimony from his daughter in court of what the abuser did to her. He had to sit across the courtroom and look at that man in the face. He had to sit through the entire court address and all of the evidence and testimony until he was given a chance to say whatever he needed to say. I knew, right at that moment, he would try and attack the man. He did. He tried. Every parent I know would have tried to do the exact same thing. He was irrational and was under a rage that some people can't understand. I can honestly say if it had been my child, my husband and I, both, would do whatever we needed to, in order to feel like justice was completely served. It's not because we feel violent or that we have that much rage coursing through our veins. It's because our fierce love for our children outweighs the rationality of our own being.

I'm sure we've all heard stories about how a child was abused and one of the parents finds the person who committed the crime. They lash out and say that they just want to "take them out back". Most people would say they'd react similarly. For myself, it would be because I couldn't imagine someone I love being harmed in such a way.

The fierce love is a very dangerous love. It's an incredible feeling to love so much. It puts a burn in your soul that you never thought would ever be real. The danger it can cause can be unpredictable if it is not controlled. Anyone in the way of that kind of love, is fiercely burned.

"Love is like a friendship caught on fire. In the beginning a flame, very pretty, often hot and fierce, but still only light and flickering. As love grows older, our hearts mature and our love becomes as coals, deep-burning and unquenchable." –Bruce Lee.

Envelope love, let it surround you, and also, let it burn deeply in your heart.

♥ 15 ♥

Friendships, living and dead.

ave you ever had those friends you wish you'd never had in the first place? I can tell you, with 100% certainty, I have. None of us know at the time. I didn't even understand people can, actually, be toxic. Future Kiyomi, if you're reading this, don't try and remember these people. You're better off! However, you did get a good lesson from them.

Once you learn how to spot those people who drowned you with their toxins, ultimately flooding your mind and time, it becomes easier to kill those friendships. If given the chance, those zombie friends will eat your brain and leave you for dead, or worse, turn you into one of them. If the latter, you become the newest victim of the virus that continues to spread.

I'll tell you a secret. It's actually alright. No doom and gloom here. Remember to forgive but not forget? This is one of those moments you can implement it. If you felt, at one point, they were a good person, but became toxic to you or any of your relationships with other people, mindfully put them on an island without a way out. If there comes a point where you feel they aren't soul suckers anymore, give them a row boat to see if they can paddle themselves and see how gently they can row.

See how many times you can implement that song into your life?

Some of the toxic friendships were actually relationships, for me. Being in a relationship is supposed to be about friends making something more. It's not supposed to be the other way around. If you aren't compatible as friends because one of you is a toxic wasteland, what makes you think that a real relationship will work? Duh! We aren't supposed to start out as a dump together then turn into a field of dreams. Or worse off, after the dump we've started with, we become a recycling center for the continuous filtering and repeat of those patterns, either with the same person, or with a new one. A healthy friendship is always a start to a solid foundation to become any type of relationship.

What's funny, I've made friendships with people I didn't know I would have such a strong connection with, since having surgery. So I guess we can find more, or different, living friendships than what we thought we had after certain situations. There are so many people who are willing to be your friend. Being in one toxic friendship, even if they have been in your life for so long, is not better than having a multitude of emotional or mental support. Quite the opposite, a toxic friend will actually encourage the destructive behavior, possibly without realizing it. This is exactly when your self reliance needs to come in. Sadly, most of the time, we don't realize stepping away is the best thing to do when we are entrapped in that relationship.

The people whom I have come to find that are my true friends, are actually people who tell me the truth without thinking twice about it. Yeah, I might get mad or upset, but in reality, they are telling me an objective opinion of something I'm obviously missing. Whether or not we want to listen, listening should still be an option. You don't have to take the advice, but I encourage you to still listen. In that friendship, if it were reversed, you would do the same thing. Golden rule here, people. Be a good friend and be supportive. Don't be destructive. However, if you see a destructive pattern or there is behavior that could be damaging, be objective, don't preach. Just ask them to take a look at what's happening and reverse the roll to you in the situation. Ask what they would say to you. I've done it with one friend in partic-ular. Encourage the ones you love, to fight for some-thing even if they want to give up. Encourage them to not settle. Notice I say encourage, not "make". Remember you can't row their boat.

I had been out with a friend for a few hours. She picked me up, we had lunch, and we decided to do our tradition to see a movie in a theatre. It takes a special friend to make time for you. Especially when they pick you up since you can't drive. It feels even more special when the destination is out of their way. She and I, honestly, haven't known each other for a long time. It doesn't seem long anyways; probably around seven years. We had gone to our movie and she was dropping me off at home. We began talking about certain personal things when I saw her start to tear up. I won't lie; most of it was probably from my "real talk" with her.

When I saw her become so sad and hurt, I couldn't imagine the pain and sadness she was feeling. I wanted to know it or to feel it, just so I could understand exactly what she needed me to do or say. All I could do was give her a hug. When we hugged, it felt like I was squeezing out her emotions. She cried and I cried. It was so cold outside, we were both shaking. We continued to stand outside, in the dark, shaking from cold, crying and hugging. She heard me, listened to what I had to say, and I know she would do the same for me, because she has.

I am so lucky to have these friends. I have friends who feel comfortable enough to care about me and feel safe with their emotions. I have friends that I can confide in and hold my deepest secrets. I can't help but feel like I'm safe in so many ways, even though, sometimes, I feel like impending doom is approaching. Watch out Mt. Everest, here I come (you'll understand this analogy soon)!

I have to mention friendships that have come in the most peculiar way. There are some friends I've never met. They've been online but we have mutual friends. Then there are some I've never met until we are with a mutual friend to have a good time together. When we get to talking, we start realizing we have a lot in common.

This first friend, however, was made when I was pregnant with Leighlan. I actually had the honor to meet her in person. If we have any mutual friends, I would be shocked and delighted. I truly don't even remember how it came about, but this woman working at a local Target became a person I have seen a heart of gold inside. The way that she was upbeat every time I saw her, the way she would ask about how the pregnancy was going, or just our plain conversations, she always had a smile on her face and a faith that would never detour.

Her faith became the most apparent to me, though, when I went into the store one day. I was starting to strike a conversation, like we always had done, and when she talked, her voice was so raspy. It sounded like she was sick. I asked if she had laryngitis or was recovering from an illness. She said no, and looked a little disappointed. It was the first time I hadn't seen her smile. She told me that she awakened one morning having trouble with her voice. She went to see the doctor. They determined she had a mass pressing against her windpipe. There was going to be a surgery and biopsy of said mass. I know she saw my upset facial expression because she said, "Don't worry. I'll be fine. I'll be fine. No matter what, it will be okay. I'll either live to see another day or I'll go home to God." I've now since changed my point of view, and my response to a lot of questions is now, "No matter what, I'll be okay". Beautiful woman.

Friendships, living and dead.

This next friend's story still makes me smile and laugh.

One day, I got a phone call from a certain satellite cable customer service agent. I had disabled service since we had moved to a different location. It was a woman and she was asking me all of her basic questions required by the company. What she hadn't known was a different agent had contacted me the week before about the same thing. Now, looking back at this, it's just hard to believe this wasn't meant to be. So we laughed because she felt bad she'd called when she didn't need to. Honestly, I can't remember the whole conversation but we were laughing and laughing. The conversation ended with exchanging information for Facebook. In 2014, I made a faceless friend. Now, because of Facebook, I can put a picture to the voice and she is so beautiful. We may or may not ever meet, but the way our conversations happen, the way she holds herself with confidence, and also the kindness she sets out into the world, I wouldn't doubt she would be a person to take you in or help you if you needed it. We are still friends. No mutual friends. We are on opposite sides of the United States, but still can retain a friendship. It's a friendship that makes me smile and I can't believe happened all because of ending my subscription to cable TV.

Now back to our regular scheduled programming.

Lessons learned, if you have some toxic zombie friends causing your life to be surrounded by chaos, just hold a funeral in your head. Zombies eat brains, don't let them eat yours or let your brains be controlled. I just went super science fiction, sorry.

Your true friends will take you to bright happy places and help you feel secure. They will be trustworthy and won't be angry when you have a multitude of support. When I say they won't be angry when you have a multitude of support, I'm mainly talking about jealousy toward your other friends. Those jealous friends will manipulate you to drop another friend so they can solely occupy all of your time. That's a vampire zombie friend. They suck you away from everyone using their false glamour powers in order to use your brains as their main course. The true friends will want to be there for you, encourage you to have as much support as possible. They will encourage you to fight, not settle. Your true friends will also let you release your dark places. They will let you cry and they will listen. Then, those friends will whip your ass back into shape and scream at you to row your own damn boat since you've started drifting toward theirs, or drifting toward that clown on the shore.

So just remember a zombie attack can happen. Your friends, who are alive and well, will help you battle your way out. Don't let your brains get eaten. I have, it hurts (pun not intended but still super funny) emotionally and mentally. It's much harder to get out of those manipulative relationships than to enter the relationship in the first place. I compare it to gluttony and then trying to diet.

Sally became friends with zombies and tried to make them happy by allowing them turn her into one. Now, Sally walks among the zombies with her half broken leg searching for other brains to join her zombie club. Don't be like Sally.

Friendships, living and dead.

"There is nothing I would not do for those who are really my friends. I have no notion of loving people by halves, it is not my nature." –Jane Austen

Let's hit the road and go on our next adventure. Maybe it will be over a mountain where you can wave at all of the zombies who can't make it up there.

♥Dad♥

Friendships, living and dead.

This is my dad. My step dad, but he's been my dad through this life. I'll be honest, I'm just going to fess up. I didn't want him anywhere near me or my family. I was a hurt child who'd just lost her father and obviously going through emotional turmoil. But he stayed. He weathered through every storm, and let me tell you I gave my parents some doozys. He worked and put food on our table. He packed my lunches that had some of the most inappropriate jokes on them. Once, one of my note drawings was taken hostage, from my lunch, by a kitchen helper. She didn't think the picture was very funny. It was a picture of Santa pooping out coal and saying I wasn't going to get any presents. I thought it was hilarious. My friends couldn't wait to see what picture he would draw in my lunch for the day. In our family, laughter was definitely what kept us sane most of the time, if not all of the time. He was really able to keep laughter alive in our house. I love him with all my heart and I'm so incredibly thankful that he chose to be my dad. For the best part? My first dad's name was Tom. My second dad's name is Jerry. So now I get to collect Tom and Jerry items whenever I find them.

1. What was your happiest moment as a child? As an adult?

Hmm.. my favorite memory was my grandpa taking me fishing. he never drove, he drove a bicycle. So he would walk up to my house, get me, he would have his fishing poles and then we would walk down to the river and fish and we would always have a sandwich.

My favorite memory as an adult is sharing all of my kids, adopted and family. Just sharing the times we joked around and helping each other with different things. all of the memories.

2. What's the most beautiful thing you've ever witnessed? What is the most beautiful thing you could give to someone else?

The most beautiful thing I've ever seen was your mom.
My farts. No just kidding. I don't know maybe I think having a sense of humor in tough times for others.

3. What makes you feel wealthy in life or love? What could you add to your life that would make you wealthier than you already are?

I think having a heart and love to share with, with those that I love and care about.
Just smiles, kids and the twinkle in their eyes, and mom's love for me. I'm pretty boring.
I want my family to know I love them, but I think they already know. Each and every one has different qualities and it's always like a little treasure from each person.

♥16♥

Mt. Everest

I'm hiking on Mt. Everest. I've no guide or anyone who knows the direction I'm supposed to be going. I'm alone and surrounding me are vast snowy peaks. At some points, a large draft of wind blows soft snow toward my face that slightly catches up my nose, causing brief air suffocation. The blast sends my arms closer to my body to try and keep myself as warm as I can. My large coat and clothes are keeping me warm as I climb up further into thinner air. I note that I need to find shelter soon to set up camp; I need rest before going on. I look at the sky and know that a stormy snow will be attacking the mountain soon. The fresh snow will be hard to walk through when it turns into a powder further up my legs. Getting a site prepared is crucial. At last, I've found some sort of cave or at least, somewhere that I can rest for a while before I continue on.

Inside the cave, it's mildly shallow. When I turn around, I can see out of the entrance, icicles hanging from the half circle outline. Another view of the snowy peaks are seen, somewhat more pleasant to witness now that I'm out of that frozen air. I begin to see the snow storm slightly blowing through and I know it will become much more serious in a matter of time.

I look around the cave dwelling and I realize I have no pack. I'm scrambling around trying to find anything that I thought I brought with me. I have no pack and no supplies. I immediately start wondering how I'm going to eat or drink anything.

I think to myself, "I can use a cooking pot and melt some snow for water".

"No, you idiot, you don't have any supplies. Go hit your head on the cave wall for that one." Apparently by this point, brain freeze has kicked in, since I'm talking to myself.

"Shh. I'm trying to think about what I'm going to do." This is the point where it's become a slushy.

I'm talking to myself, no supplies, stuck in a cave on Mt. Everest, and now I have gone mad. Put me down, save Yeller!

To torture myself further, I've just realized I'm on Mt. Everest, in a cave, no pack, no supplies, no water, no food...and now, I'm NAKED! I was clothed before but to just make this harder to survive, how about I have all of my lumps, bumps, humps, and holes out?! How am I supposed to keep warm? That's it, I'm going to die in a cave on Mt. Everest, freaking naked.

Somehow, I'm Doctor Who and have transported to the Grand Canyon. Beautiful isn't it? It's a much better view than Mt. Everest and much warmer, too.

Thankfully, I have all of my clothes on, this time. The canyon looks like carvings that were made into a painting by Bob Ross.

I'm immediately broken from my trance to find out that my kids are hanging over the ledge. I run and lunge my body toward the edge of the cliff and grab them, one child dangling from each hand. I'm slowly slipping further to the edge since the ground beneath me is sandier than being in friction. I start to wonder how I'm going to get both of them up and save us all.

BAM!

I'm on a bridge. My kids are in the backseat. We're all strapped in. The windows are up since it's a warm day and I have the air-conditioner on. Instantly, we are pulled from our trip down memory lane with a song we all love, when the bridge begins to fall into pieces beneath us. I know we're about to fall into water and I have no idea how I'm going to get all of us out safely. We start sinking into the water and I unbuckle all of us while trying to still get a door or window open so we can slide out easily.

I don't get to the end of any of these scenarios. They all end with an open ending. Mainly because I just don't want to know the ending. I think I pull myself out on purpose just so I stay on some sort of ground, or my bed, which is where a lot of these anxieties come into play. Writing all of those made my palms sweat. These scenarios are things that play in my mind. Future Kiyomi, hopefully this has diminished a little.

I call these scenarios, "Being on Mt. Everest". I invent myself into these high intensity situations where I'm helpless. The lack of control is what makes me fall into that state, but my strength of my subconscious control keeps my endings open. It's amazing what the human brain can do.

At night, these are what come into my mind. I have much more gruesome screenplays in my head but those are saved when I'm at a very low point and have to immediately get my mind somewhere else.

I've learned that these terrible control issues mainly happen after appointments where I fear what may lie ahead or when I'm left to feel insecure and powerless. I've learned a way on how to control them.

"Are you on Mt. Everest?"

"No."

"Are you planning to go to Mt. Everest?"

"No."

"If you go to Mt. Everest, will you be unprepared as well as be naked?"

"No."

"Where do you live? What day is it? Where are you right at this very moment?"..."What's your name, who's your daddy?" I had to throw that in there.

These are questions I ask myself to bring me back to my real reality. If I start to feel myself slip again, I repeat it, but it continues to happen, I know I'm in a loop. Once I'm in a loop, I find a feel-good-show or book is the ticket. It takes my mind off of the moment and I absorb into what I'm focusing on.

Mt. Everest is something I'm exposing and is vulnerable for me. I've talked to several other people who have similar instances of putting themselves in situations of fear and lack of control. We've officially named it "Mt. Everest". It makes it much easier for everyone to know what we call it so when we need each other, we know exactly what it means when we say we're up a mountain naked.

Thinking of these things is so hard to put into words. You lose yourself in the moment. You begin to feel like nothing around you is anything other than what you see in your own head. It's not even real, yet you're there, experiencing the moment of anxiety and panic.

If you experience these things, as well, I hope with all of my heart you are able to get out of them. It's a form of torture, mentally.

I thought I was alone with this. My aunt and I will write each other, since we're in different time zones, and we'll get it the next morning.

"I was on Mt. Everest and it was freezing and somehow my naked body was stuck to some ice." The worse we feel, the more exaggerated we get with Mt. Everest. Sometimes we have gear, sometimes not.

My friend, after I explained what Mt. Everest was, she told me hers was also the fear of the water with her kids. I was astonished it was a fear close to mine.

You are not alone, no matter what type of situation happens in your mind. You aren't alone. You may be alone in the Amazon being devoured by piranhas in your head, but in reality, we are all here facing some storm or another.

Remember, we never know our true strength until we are at the mercy of our weakness.

Make your open ending, survival.

"The greatest weapon against stress is our ability to choose one thought over another." –William James

❤17❤

Dreaming and Ambition

Remember our discussion about never settling? Remember how we talked about living the life that will make you happy, and live for that? This is the child of that chapter.

The dreaming of my future actually started in my childhood years, as most of us. I dreamed of being so many things. I told my mom I wanted to be in the WNBA, I wanted to be the first woman president, be an astronaut to see the whole world at once, and be the one who works in Africa or other countries giving to those in need. I had pictured administering vaccinations to children or working in the orphanage of children who had H.I.V. Talk about dreams... I had some huge ones. Not only did I have those dreams, but I felt like I had the ambition to do them. I never once thought to myself I couldn't do those things. I even told myself I could be all of those things at the same time. I reached for the stars and wanted to be great. I think most of all; I wanted to be remembered somehow, in a great way. Maybe not famously, but to have done something great.

What were your dreams as a child? What was it that you thought you wanted to be, no matter what? I know that dreams change as we get older. We start to change what our likes and dislikes become. Much like how they say our taste buds change every seven years, our taste for our dreams changes a little bit, or completely.

When I envisioned someone who inspired me, more than anyone, I thought of MLK, Jr. I love everything MLK, Jr. stood for. Every aspect he was, he represented, mesmerized my thoughts. I devoured the words he spoke in his sermons. I've read several which are written down and listened to the ones recorded. They were so beautifully and thoughtfully said. I tear up and feel that my mind trying to comprehend how profound each word was. He spoke eloquently and most of the time, I felt a sense of peace from reading each word he spoke. Some of us may not have been around to actually hear those words in person, but to read them is still a closeness I crave. His dream was equality, peace, and love. His dream was acted out in the bravest way. He became vulnerable. He became the advocate for so many who saw his dream and believed in it. The most wonderful thing I think about, especially when he spoke publicly, he wasn't just talking about our darker skinned family, there were lighter skinned family there supporting him and the equality he spoke. Black and white didn't matter in the moment. What mattered was that anyone who was there, was in support of love and equality.

"Someone on the T.V. said that the other guy was black but there is no black and there is no white of people. We all just look like different shades of brown." That is what my six year old son said to me. I've taken that to heart. My son and daughter never mentioned anything about different skin color. Race was never raised in our family. Equality and love were our main focus.

This year, on MLK, Jr. day, the kids asked why it was a holiday. We homeschool so we have the privilege to educate them on the basis of when it's important for them to ask. This was the perfect opportunity to discuss the important, but compacted version of history. Since they are so young, we put it into a way they were better able to understand. I showed them videos of MLK, Jr. and how he wanted everyone to be treated with love and respect. When my husband and I told our children he had been murdered for wanting love and respect for people who were seen as different, they began to cry. When we tried to explain to them sometimes people are afraid of people who are different or what they don't understand, they looked as though they just couldn't comprehend why this would be our world. My husband explained how some people who were darker brown were killed just because of how their skin looked. The hurt, terror, and anger on their faces was so disheartening. It was the part of life we all have stolen from us at some point. It's the part where you have the rainbows and sunshine ripped away from your heart.

"That's a bully! If someone ever did that, I would say to them that they can't treat someone like that just because they are different!" My son had a lump in his throat as he said it. His little mouth was turned down slightly and you could see the tears starting to well up. There was another instance where my son said someone was a bully, but it had not been mentioned of the color of their skin. He sees the movement of their heart and the quality of their actions, not the skin color of who is involved.

I'm truly thankful for being able to teach my children the importance of equality and love. I'm thankful for them to understand how people act is what matters most about a person. I'm thankful that among the hate of the world, they will grow up in the understanding of love and kindness. They will grow up not just with a dream, but also with the action of continuing love and kindness through their life. I will support them in that, if I'm unable to do anything else.

To dream, not in the sense of sleep, is to contemplate the possibility of doing something. Any dream that does not involve harming any being, is important. It does not matter what it is. If you're a child and see a grocery bagger and think, yep, that's what I want to be. Then go right ahead and let that be your ambition to guide you to your dream.

With everything I'm saying, I want you to know I will support you.

I actually made a video a few years back. It was about having a dream and making the ambition for you to accomplish it. I laughed at what I said. I hadn't even remembered it, just until recently when I watched it over. I went on about how whatever dream or ambition you had, I would support you. Even if I was the only person in your life that would support it, I would support you.

"If you have a goal or a dream and you want to try to achieve it, then I will support you. I 100% will support you. If you want to be a fish, I'll go make you some fins. I will go make you some fins and I will drive you to the beach and I'll watch you swim your little heart out because you know what? You are still closer to achieving that goal than if you hadn't tried at all. So my encouragement for today is to be you. Be a fish, I don't care. I'll love you anyways."

That is word for word what I said. Having a dream doesn't just mean sitting there wishing it would happen. It's also about having that AMBITION to do it! You cannot expect something to happen if you aren't even willing to try. I had made another video on getting out of your comfort zone. Getting out of your comfort zone is scary sometimes. You might be hesitant. One thing I had taken away from the second video was when I said, "If you do not step out of that comfort zone and try, I guarantee you **will** fail".

"It's all about self development. It's if you're willing to stay in the spot that you are, with just content, or you had the choice to be content or be extremely happy with living your life day to day and experiencing the joy that life has. It's so precious. We are so mortal. We are so temporary. Take a chance. Take a chance in this life. Take a chance with things that you want to experience. Just step out of your comfort zone and embrace it."

Dreaming and Ambition

Some of these videos, I barely remember. Actually, I don't think I remember them at all. I watch them and I ask myself who that was. I watch them and I agree with them, almost as if I'm watching someone else. It helps me to remember to be motivated and be happy.

The point is if you have the ambition to accomplish your dreams, you can slowly do it. If you choose to not do it, it's not because of anything or anyone else. There is no one to blame for any of it. It's you. It's your choice and lack of ambition. Just try. I can guarantee you'll absolutely fail if you do not even try.

I told you about my "midnight writes". It's my private journal about message dreams. It also has quotes I think of in the night. Before I used it as my journal, I wrote everything into the front cover that inspired me to start the journal in the first place. All of the quotes I wrote into the cover are all about dreaming. Not just about actual dreams that are involved with sleep, but dreaming about the world or about what I wish people could be when they make their dream. I'll be vulnerable and share it with you. So, here we go. Are you ready?

"The future belongs to those who believe in the beauty of their dreams" –Eleanor Roosevelt.

"You have to dream before your dreams can come true." –A.P.J. Abdul Kalam.

"To accomplish great things, we must not only act, but also dream; not only plan, but also believe." –Anatole France.

"There are those who look at things the way they are, and ask why. I dream of things that never were, and ask why not?" –Robert Kennedy.

"Dreams must be heeded and accepted. For a great many of them are true." –Paracelsus.

"All our dreams can come true, if we have the courage to pursue them." –Walt Disney.

"Every great dream begins with a dreamer. Always remember, you have within you the strength, the patience, and the passion to reach for the stars to change the world." –Harriet Tumbman.

"Deep into that darkness peering, long I stood there, wondering, fearing, doubting, dreaming dreams no mortal ever dared to dream before." –Edgar Allan Poe.

"I close my eyes, then I drift away, into the magic night I softly say, a silent prayer, like the dreamers do, then I fall asleep to dream my dreams of you." –Roy Orbison.

"If one advances confidently in the direction of his dreams, and endeavors to live the life which he has imagined, he will meet with a success unexpected in common hours." –Henry David Thoreau.

Lastly, "Who looks outside, dreams; who looks inside, awakes." –Carl Jung.

I started the first page of that journal on May 23rd, 2015. This was just a month after the diagnosis of the brain tumor.

The dreaming and ambition of this life, it will keep you motivated and will keep you going. I dream of a life where pain does not come daily, or even all day long. My ambition is to constantly try whatever I can to alleviate it, even if it's just a little bit. This is only a personal dream. I have so many I wish and hope for and the best thing I can do for myself is to try.

As Superman said, "Dreams save up. Dreams lift us up and transform us. And on my soul I swear, until my dream of a world where dignity, honor, and justice becomes the reality we all share, I'll *never* stop fighting. Ever".

"You're much stronger than you think you are. Trust me". –Superman.

For the sake of this chapter, be a fish.

♥Momma♥

Dreaming and Ambition

This woman has been a constant support in my entire life. Even from a young age I went through a lot of medical issues and because she is a mother, she never settled. She fought for me and I truly knew it. Even though I was young, I knew she fought for me. Life could not have chosen a better mother for me to have through everything our family endured. I wanted to be a mother because of what kind of mother she was to me. The songs she would sing me when I was little are the same songs I sing to my kids. Throughout this book I've said, "My mom has said" and should be proof that momma is always right. A parent isn't just a parent. They are a teacher. They are an example and to help you move forward without making dumbass mistakes. She didn't have a good upbringing at all. Hers was a story of hardship and abuse. Her mindset just shows how strong she is since she decided to break the cycle and show love and patience to us when it could have been a completely different way. It's given her children a chance to raise her grandchildren in a way that will filter down through generations. Thank you, momma. I love you so much.

1. What was your happiest moment as a child? As an adult?

Laying on the grass looking up at the blue sky and fluffy white clouds. as an adult realizing how much God loves me.

2. What's the most beautiful thing you've ever witnessed? What is the most beautiful thing you could give to someone else?

The birth of children—my own and others. the most beautiful thing i can give to another is my time—it is finite and the only thing that is truly mine.

3. What makes you feel wealthy in life or love? What could you add to your life that would make you more wealthy than you already are?

Laughter makes me feel wealthy. there is nothing else except someone sharing their gift of time with me that could make me feel wealthier.

❤18❤

Happiness

I was recently talking to a friend about happiness. I brought up a moment, I remembered, when my husband and I had gone through counseling. We discussed how we cannot make the other person feel how we are feeling. This also translated into not being able to make the other person feel happy. Our counselor had said we can give love, respect, kindness, and forgiveness, but can't make another person happy.

When he said that, I could not believe I've never thought about that before. Did that sink in for you? Read it again if you need to. It's so true. It went right into my gut. I never thought to realize my happiness stems from myself. I am the responsibility, the self reliance, and the ambition, to make my own self, happy.

I had happiness written down on my little notepad of one of the topics I wanted to discuss. I had this whole other thing planned out about how happiness is so important to your life and blah, blah, blah. However, when I saw that video, my mind went crazy with thoughts. At first, I was almost blowing off the statement and about to call B.S. Then, for that brief second before he explained, my mind switched into rowing my own boat.

You, **you**, you cannot make someone else happy. No matter how much time, love, devotion, kindness, forgiveness, and plans for your future together, you can never give them their own happiness. That state of mind comes from them! Can you believe this?! I'm having a huge revelation. I don't know about you, but my mind is blown!

The recent events of our world have left us so divided. Remember, we are selfish beings. We believe our happiness survives in someone else. The first example that comes into mind is people who use a revolving door from relationship to relationship, expecting some sort of happiness to come out of it. Those new relationships aren't going to give you anything except a lesson. Then when it fails, it's up to you to figure out if you've learned from it. You row your own boat. Don't expect someone else to just say, "Here is some happiness in the form of an ore I thought you might need". It just doesn't work that way. It ends up being, "I'm just not happy anymore" or "You don't make me happy anymore". First of all, the first statement has absolutely nothing to do with you. That's their own problem they need to sort through. Paddle your little kayak into the beautiful, merrily stream. The second, again, you can have kindness and love and it may still not be enough for that person to be happy with you.

I was so angry at so many things through these last few years. No matter what, I'd allow myself some time to just thrive in those moments where I wanted to drop kick that bitch lady doctor. Then, within some time, I'd be with my family and my focus was being consumed with happiness. I was happy to be with them and have fun. My own emotion, my own boat, I was happy and at peace. Even if it was only for brief moments, I knew where my happiness was.

I have to tell you, sometimes I tell my kids the title of the "chapter". I then ask what they think about what the words mean to them. This time, I asked my son and daughter what they thought of when I said the word "Happiness". My daughter said that she feels happy when she's with her family. My son stated that same comment, but then added something I hadn't thought of.

"When I think of happiness, I think of being free." What? A six year old had a mindset that just blew me away.

Being free is also an act of self direction. If you think about it, being free is to have control over yourself, which is what we've been talking about this whole time! It's self reliance, it's control over not accepting what someone else says about you, it's forgiving, it's dreaming, it's friendships you choose to keep, it's being an individual, it's choosing to give kindness, and it's how you choose your future. Being free is the single act of bringing your own happiness to yourself.

What a revelation. My wish, right now, is to hold onto this moment. I want to remember my happiness is what I make it. My being free is how I choose it to be. It's wonderful to think, even in the inevitable end, you can have a choice of what you want.

I never thought our own selves have so much control. My mind is running a million miles right now. It's almost like someone just handed me the entire universe with all of the galaxies and told me to take responsibility for all of it. Lord help us all! For all of you, hold onto your gravity because I already know I could screw things up for you really quickly.

I don't know what part of this entire book you will feel that resonated with you, but there are a few for me I just can't believe I've never thought of before. I'm glad I'm telling you all of this. Hopefully by now, if you're reading this, you will know what I'm sharing in this book are things important to me. They've been things I feel have impacted my life. I hope there is something in this book you can relate to. I don't want you to feel alone. I would love for you to have your happiness.

"I wish, as well as everybody else, to be perfectly happy; but, like everybody else, it must be in my own way." –Jane Austen

Let me stop here, because I'm the boss........ of myself.

♥ 19 ♥

Extraordinary

Since we have so much control over ourselves, including our individuality and our happiness, it's only fitting to go the extra mile and become extraordinary.

I've heard people say striving to be extraordinary takes away from the ordinary things of life. Again, I call bullshit.

Remember the movie, "The Jungle Book"? The song called "Bare Necessities" talks about how to look for only the ordinary things that will help you just get by. Remember we talked about just being "content" instead of making a decision to be more than happy? There is a lyric in that song that just makes me shake my head.

"And don't spend your time lookin' around,
For something you want that can't be found."

Being extraordinary is not just being content with being ordinary. It's being individual. Being ordinary automatically makes me think that someone isn't willing to do that little bit "extra". Doing the same thing over and over again is nothing other than accepting that you've been given a shitty hand and you just have to deal with it.

NO!

There is a world beyond your tiny little bed of pity. How do you know something can't be found if you DON'T spend your time looking around? If you know who Indiana Jones is, he explored things many told him weren't real or it was a waste of time. Granted, he was a fictional character, but he was extraordinary because he did search for something because if he hadn't, what do you think he'd have felt? Regret, folks. Regret. This obviously goes along with dreaming and ambition, so he became our fictional "fish". Plus, he would have stories of adventure even if he never found anything.

If you go through life thinking you are ordinary or told that you are ordinary, you'll most likely live ordinary. Remember, don't let someone tell you, who you are.

My children have been asked questions so that they can tell me the affirmations they've learned, which I've taught them. I ask them their name which is where it all starts. They tell me their name, they are beautiful, they are kind, they are extraordinary, and when I ask why, they say, "Because I can change the world".

I don't accept us as an ordinary family. We have gone through extraordinary things. The most important thing my husband and I have taught our kids, is life is a gift. They've been given the gift of life.

Extraordinary

So on our birthdays, especially our children's birthdays, we ask what they would like to gift to the world, for giving them the gift of life. They've done charity, giving to the animal shelter, the food bank, homeless donations, and have given gifts from the angel trees at Christmas. They get a gift from my husband and family, usually. The hardest thing that we've had to tell them we couldn't do, was adopt a whole bunch of kids who've needed homes. My son was devastated and cried all day long. My daughter is such an animal lover, she sobs when she sees videos of mother animals being reunited with their babies, even though it's a happy ending. Through her sobs she manages to piece together a sentence, "This is so Be-U-full".

I'm proud of my kids. I'm proud I am teaching them to be extraordinary. Being extraordinary is a decision you want to make about yourself. Even if you choose to be ordinary, it's still something you *chose* and not forced into.

"The need for more is contagious. Therefore, one of the greatest gifts you can give your children is an appreciation for being content with what they have… but not with who they are." –Unknown

Don't be ordinary, when you can give that little extra.

♥Lee♥

Extraordinary

I met Lee at our local shopping market, where she works. It's a small little grocery store, where everyone knows your name. She was my very first Happy Beautiful Wealthy person. Since then, I get to see her with a smile on her face and she always gets to tell me what's up in her life. Her "interview" took place just days before her husband was having a major medical procedure done with his heart that would determine a lot of other things for them. I was able to take their photo since they hadn't had one in many years. I loved being able to get to know her and chat with her. Her story impacted me so much that I cried and cried because I kept rereading it.

1. What is my happiest moment as a child?

Sadly it was when I gave birth to my daughter, at 14. Our family was dysfunctional. My parents separated a few times. My mother emptied out the checking account, took my little sister and I to Utah. Because I was pregnant at 13, she made me tell people I was 18 and my husband was in the military. At one point a couple asked if they could adopt my child, and when I said no, they asked what could you possibly give this child? I said love. My mother was a nut case. She abused us when she was mad. While pregnant she pulled a dog's chain in front of me and I fell. I had a series of false labor pains until she was born. My mother faked a suicide attempt, the bank repossessed the truck and somehow we ended up in the middle of the desert in a motel. When my mother had 2 guys in the room and locked us out, I ran to the highway and hitched a ride with a truck driver, whom tried to molest me and when we stopped at a truck stop I told someone there. Some guys went looking for him but he scooted. They all got up cab money to the airport as I thought I had a plane ticket to my dad's ready. After being there for hours, a black man approached me and ultimately informed everyone there he was taking me home and would make sure I was on a plane for home the next day. He washed my clothes, let me bathe and then made me call my dad. The very next day I was headed home to Portland.

1. What is my happiest moment as an adult?

I must say when my husband and I fell in love. We had known the same circle of friends, and our paths never crossed. I met him at a local restaurant, so I knew him a little. He showed up at my door around 1am. We talked until 7am. He was saying he was going to his bosses cabin and would I like to go? There was nothing creepy about him, but I figured he wouldn't show up later, but he did! So I went for the weekend and I knew after 4 days that this was the man of my dreams.

2.What is the most beautiful thing I've ever witnessed?

The birth of my grand children..hands down. What do I feel is the most beautiful thing I could give to someone else?
Love. I wasn't raised in a very loving home. I once asked my dad why there was no love in our home. He said there was, we just didn't know how to show it. To this day, I'm kind of hard on the outside. I have a tough exterior.. lol. I rarely had to spank my kids, because I had the "look". I honestly didn't think my dad knew I existed until my little sister died in a car accident. That's when he said to me that you should go before your kids. We became pretty close in the years that followed. I lost my dad suddenly and I was devastated. I was estranged from my mother for nine years prior to her death. When I did learn of her death I shed a tear only because she was my mother, but felt little else. When I think about my dad I cry. But not my mother. Am I a freak?

3. What makes me feel wealthy in life or love?

I have my very best friend at my side. We were meant to be, I just wish we had met sooner than we did. We took in 3 kids that had nowhere to go, no stability, no future. We were planning to move 3000 miles away. Together we raised 5 kids and at times it was pure hell.

HeARTwork

What could I add to my life that would make me feel more wealthy than I already am?

To finally finish my house so I can enjoy it! I've been living out of boxes for 26 yrs. We have 8 yrs left on our mortgage, and adding some financial freedom would enrich me a lot!

My husband and I are a team. We work well together and love spending time together. We appreciate each other's need to do our own thing. Our roles have reversed, now he's the stay at home "parent" while I work, even though I too have always worked. I understand his frustration with that role. All too well! We watch out for one another. When I'm sick he nurses me back and vice versa. We'll celebrate 29 yrs this Dec. Hard to believe we made it. What doesn't kill us, only makes us stronger.

♥ 20 ♥

Laughter

I'm hoping you're still here with me. This one, laughter, is one of the more important things I want to write about. It may get silly and it may get dejected. I don't want this point to detour you off of this course.

First of all, I know what you've gone through. We all have struggles, and remember, we don't compare ourselves to others. So, I know what you've gone through; you've gone through struggles. I'm so sorry. There is nothing we can do in this world that will ever take that away. What's done is done. It can't be changed. No matter what, someone will experience a miserable moment.

I want to understand this. I still strive to understand this. I hope you follow me. Being in the moment of life can bring you joy and it can bring you sadness. My mom has always said that we never have bad days, just bad moments. I've held that in my mind and in my heart especially when the day has been heavy. The most heavily weighted and bad moment in that day can make you feel like time could not exist right now. You don't see an end with all of the weights strapped to your feet and have no destination in front of you. There has to be some sort of rewind or some sort of stop button. It doesn't. It never does. I'm sorry for that. I can't control it either. I wish I could, for you, for me, for the world. It just never stops. I'm just so sorry. I know the feeling.

In that moment, where you feel like time cannot exist, the deepest parts of our soul can think of something special or good. I know that that seems impossible with the circumstance. I know that feeling all too well. However, when I look back, I can think of wonderful things through a hard or sorrowful moment. Think about a moment where time needed to rewind, stop, or fast forward. Now, think about a good piece that came out of it. It's hard, but we can still do it with a grain of salt in our mouths.

No matter through death, loss, or life, we will have those memories. We have what we remember of the good things. It could be that you've still been given life apart from a traumatic circumstance. It could be that you're grateful to have memories of someone whom you loved dearly, that has long since passed. It could be that every day you wake, you still have breath to see it. No matter the circumstance, there can be a moment of a happy memory.

Sometimes it's painful to think about those things. It is for me still.

Do you remember the saying, "Laughter is the best medicine"? I actually thought about that and it seriously pissed me off. I think that I just had to be angry at something and whenever I heard it or read it from someone; I wanted to punch them in the face or rip them through the computer screen. It seemed like the biggest load of crap I'd heard amidst something terrible I was going through. I was being selfish, we just can't help it.

If you can, remember this. Remember this among the tragedy or sorrow you are experiencing. There will be a time that you will be able to think of something, or someone will say something to you, where a little chuckle may come out. Don't stay in your dark tunnel just because you want to. Listen to the moment and allow the chuckle. For that single moment where you allow any type of happiness come through to you, there is a slight feeling of light. I'm not saying you go into full on laughter on the floor. You will, however, be letting in the tiny, miniscule, atom sized piece of healing into your heart and mind.

Time will continue and the feeling of despair will stay. Being honest here, it usually never goes away but it may just slide in and out. Sometimes there will be days where it's sweeping over your eyes and it just seems to be everywhere. That's alright. The days that you aren't cuddled in bed weeping, may be where a smile makes its way through. There is a song I sing, even to my kids when they can get so upset.

Smile, though your heart is aching,
Smile, even though it's breaking.
When there are clouds in the sky,
You'll get by.
If you smile, through your fear and sorrow,
Smile, and maybe tomorrow,

You'll see the sun come shining through,
For you, light up your day with gladness.
Hide, every trace of sadness.
Although a tear, may be ever so near,
That's the time
You must keep on trying.
Smile, what's the use in crying?
You'll find that life is still worthwhile.
If you'll just, smile.

The instrumental song was composed in a film by Charlie Chaplin, and then John Turner and Geoffrey Parsons wrote the lyrics. The composure makes it sound mournful at times, and then the lyrics make it powerful. That's life, so much. With every ounce of horrible, there is a moment worth living.

You may not be able to laugh at the moment, but just smiling is good enough. Remember, if you can't do anything, just stand up.

After everything that has happened, laughter has actually been one of my greatest comforts, even if I wanted to scoff at the notion.

My husband, at every appointment, would try so much to be witty and funny. He knew I wanted to bolt for my life, cover my ears, close my eyes, and somehow find my way out of whatever hospital or appointment I was at. I would try to climb Mt. Everest. Matt would have to look for me everywhere and I would shout from the mountain top, "Yo-del-eh-Hee-HOO!". Every single time, though, I would laugh. He made it happen.

A funny time, we both remember vividly, was literally the day coming home from the hospital after brain surgery. It really wasn't so funny at the moment. We can laugh about it now, though. I had a pillow against the window and I was on pain meds. My face was swollen and it looked like I'd been beaten with some sort of metal pipe. My eye was swollen shut and everything from my scalp down to my upper lip, was black, blue, and purple. There could have been some green so I'm not entirely sure. Matt was in a carpool lane, driving, but then realizes he has accidentally gone off of a left hand exit.

He says, "Well, we need gas anyways".

We drive off of the freeway; he makes some sort of turn into the middle of nowhere. I kid you not; he drove for an hour out of the way, where we finally found an AMPM gas station. I had to use the bathroom by the end of it. No gas, having to pee, in horrible pain, all while lacking civilization driving for an hour in "Deliverance" land. I may be exaggerating a little.

We arrive at the gas station, to get gas, and for me to use the bathroom. Of course when I get to the bathroom door, I need a key. So I go into the little store, looking like a zombie, ask for the bathroom key, and leave to do my business. I felt like I was about to get a flesh eating virus sitting in that bathroom with the staples in my head. When I came out, a woman was standing there, just in front of the door to where she wouldn't be hit when it opened. She had been waiting for the bathroom key. She stood there looking absolutely horrified. I couldn't see out of my right eye, so I turned and tilted my head. I looked like "Sloth" from the "Goonies" movie mixed with a little of a zombie horror film. Her breath caught, along with her hand palming against her chest, I'm sure out of horror. Truly I'm surprised she didn't shriek.

Matt had been waiting for me near the bathroom along the curb. I handed the poor, horrified, woman the key to the bathroom. She spots Matt, almost pleading for an explanation of why Zombie Sloth has come to life from an AMPM bathroom. Matt says, "Oh, she just had brain surgery and we are on our way home". I can be almost certain she was planning on calling the police. The swat team would have surrounded us and Matt would have had to bend over, once in custody. I really can't say in that moment, I would have been too upset about it.

All I could think of was getting my pain meds soon, since I had a paper prescription to drop off. I wish I'd had some to take so I didn't have to talk or listen to him the rest of the car ride home. I was so mad. I should have written "PLEH" on the car window so the woman would have driven me to the freeway. That same freeway that Matt couldn't seem to find. If you don't know what "PLEH" is, read it backwards.

This was not something we could laugh about then. Partly because I had staples in my head and I'd probably become a staple gun from the pressure of laughing, but also because it was not funny not having pain meds after having that kind of surgery, 3 days prior.

At this point, every time we pass the exit, coming home from all of the hospitals, we laugh. He asks me every time if I'd like to take a road trip. Sometimes I give him the "really" stare, and sometimes we just start talking about it and laugh.

Laughter

Apart from some hard and unknown things, I can laugh and think about something even when it wasn't a great moment that happened in that period of time. I bet that lady wasn't laughing.

I know this won't be funny to some people, but there was an appointment before February 8th, where it had me so stressed out. I knew the next appointment would be about February 8th, and would be what we'd be discussing. I just kept replaying what had happened in the office and what we'd be discussing. We were leaving the hospital and Matt knew I was in my head, somewhere, who knows where. Well, I know where, and now we all know where I go under anxiety circumstances. Don't forget some supplies when you meet me at the top of the mountain.

When we talk about the seizures or about all of the other things encompassing around our walls, he usually will call me a potato throughout the sentence. In particular, after this appointment, he thought he would be so witty. This type of extreme witty, from him, is usually saved for the very serious appointments where I get the most upset.

There was a show called, "Flipper", about a dolphin. Seems weird to just spring that out of nowhere, but let me explain. As we start to get onto the on-ramp of the freeway to finally voyage our way through traffic to go home, he says, "Instead of Potato, I can call you Flopper, Flipper's epileptic cousin".

We were both laughing so hard Matt had missed our turn off of the exit. Instead, we went in a circle and had to reenter from where we had started. We then started laughing about missing the exit because of "Flopper". Then the AMPM story came up. We joked how he was probably just going to pull off of random exits just to piss me off. This led to uncontrollable laughter and he missed the exit a second time! He says he missed the second exit because he couldn't see from all of the tears in his eyes from laughing. My stomach and face were hurting from having my mouth too wide open, and the constant crunch my stomach muscles were in. That was my exercise.

This month I'm writing, it's mine and my husband's 12th wedding anniversary, and we'll have been together for 13 years as a couple. We've had our trials. Marriage is not for the faint hearted, especially when you make that commitment knowing you are going in with the mindset you will not leave. Obviously, it's all based on circumstances. Matt has continued to be my support.

Sorrow and laughter can come from all things. However, I will have to accept the sorrow, but I will embrace the laughter. Even if it's in an AMPM bathroom.

"Laughter has no foreign accent." –Paul Lowney.

♥ 21 ♥

Faith

I've told you, I'm not super interested about talking religion with you, my friends. This isn't so much about religion, as it is about faith. They are two completely separate entities.

Religion for people, who are religious, is a place of sanctuary where they can worship their own personal God. No matter what religion or God it may be.

Faith, to me, is believing something will be how you want it to be. It doesn't mean you know for sure it's going to be that way. It means you have a piece of hope someone else may not have. Anyone can have faith. It's universal. Just like love.

When I have had little faith about the aspect of things that have happened and what may occur, I find faith in little ways. I write to my aunt, who is in Scotland, nearly every day. I keep her updated with everything that's happening and we talk about how we wish that my Scotland trip was sooner. She uplifts me mentally, a lot of the time, and is always on my side until she tells me I'm wrong and she's right.

When I started having the seizures all day long, I was scheduled to leave for Scotland April 25th, 2017. I had to cancel the Scotland trip the day before I was supposed to leave, because of the seizures. I was heartbroken. I cried and was so angry about not being able to visit the one place I've ever wanted to travel. I've still been so disappointed about that and I wish so badly I could go. I tell her how much fear I have about not being able to come if something were to go wrong. She always tells me the time will come and we will know it.

Even when I'm on Mt. Everest, my faith can always be reassured when someone hears me and I get the affirmation I need so I'm not naked and stranded. The headspace of faith while on Mt. Everest is very hard to come back into. It's when I know myself enough to reconfigure my emotions and talk to someone. Sometimes it helps to get another opinion.

I do get fooled very easily. I will admit, sometimes I trick myself into believing I have faith, when I really don't. Or, at least not as much as I want. Yep, I fell dumb to the "victim" of "I can't because of bleh blah bleh". I want to be able to have faith over everything. I want to be able to see the positive outcome of my visions. Faith isn't something that just comes to us. It's something we can control. Duh. Isn't that what I've been telling myself through this whole thing?

More than just having faith in myself, I want to have faith in people. Has anyone else noticed how separated our country is and how much people have changed? I don't speak of any side. I speak of just in general. I really want to have faith in people and I know I can control that. However, I just don't know if I'm being naive at this point.

There are adults and kids eating washing machine liquid, bath salts, smoking fruit loops, putting fur on their nails, and having so many injections that they start looking like they have an ass for a face. I just don't get it. Oh, I've also seen those weird snake eyebrows and they make it part of their lips now. I'll admit that some are less severe than others. Still, WHAT THE HELL, PEOPLE?!

Faith in humanity is slowly diminishing from my point of view and from a lot of other's. It's so sad our future people to run this world when we're gone, are seeing what cleaning solution can do to their insides.

I think that the only faith in humanity I will put my energy into is my children. I have faith while they will still make mistakes, they will learn from those mistakes, and they won't be eating cleaning solution or smoking things that shouldn't be inhaled. I have faith they will make good decisions throughout their life and for their (common sense) family.

"The meaning of faith is not to live in the heavens, but to settle heaven in your heart." –Thomas Hardy

However, I will choose to have faith that no matter the life, the life will matter.

❤Debbie❤

Faith

I actually met Debbie through my husband, Matt. They'd gone to school together and had reconnected. The funny part of it all, Debbie and I would talk all the time in text messages. But we hadn't met and it didn't really hit us until we did her photo session. It was like we'd known each other for so long that it didn't feel like we'd never met. She's one of my very good and close friends now. We do a lot of venting and problem solving. I just love her to pieces.

1. What was your favorite memory as a child? As an adult?

My happiest moment as a child was fishing with my Dad. Just him and I all day on this little wooden dock on Loomis Lake at Long Beach Washington. My absolute favorite memory is when Alyssa my oldest daughter held Emma my youngest daughter for the first time. Emma was only an hour old and Alyssa rushed to my bed to be the first one to hold her baby sister. She sang to Emma and told her she was going to protect her and love her forever.

2. What is the most beautiful thing you have ever witnessed? What's the most beautiful thing you could give to someone else?

The most beautiful thing I have ever witnessed was my nephew meeting each one of my girls after they were born. He was so happy and excited, the most beautiful thing I could give anyone would be my heart. My strength is what makes me feel Beautiful, even when I doubt myself I always muster up the strength to find the positive side of my situation at hand and the motivation to grow in times of darkness.

3. What makes you feel most wealthy in life or love? What could you add to your life that would make you feel wealthier than you already are?

My family is what makes me wealthy, I have been extremely blessed to have the love and support of my family and friends whom I consider to be my family. Adding independence to my life would add to my wealth.

♥ 22 ♥

Family

"**F**irst comes love, and then comes marriage."
There's a reason love comes first. A family isn't
just about people who have relative blood rushing
through their veins. Family begins with love. It's what
holds it and what nurtures the love to grow.

Have you heard of the saying, "Blood is thicker
than water"? This saying is usually talking about how
blood family is more important than a family that
you've accepted or chosen. When I did a little digging,
I found out a fun little fact. The actual saying is, "The
blood of the covenant is thicker than the water of the
womb". Which means, not only has that saying been
turned around, but also that the meaning was turned
around as well. Instead, it's saying that the family we
choose to be our family is thicker than just the people
who have birthed us from their veins.

I have several networks of families. I have friends
and their parents who I'm close to. I have people

whom I've known all my life that I can consider my actual close family. I know if I ask something of any person that's in my network of family, one of them would be there. They know if they needed anything, someone would be there for them. It's an amazing connection when you can have that with someone other than being just your biological family.

The family you create should be the people who build you up and who support you through anything. They should be people you are proud to be around and who you feel like are positive influences that can get through turmoil.

Since the moment of April of 2015 to right now, the thoughts of my everyday life are of my family. They are what get me through the day. They are who support me and who allow me to be myself. I always have a support system and encouragement. Family is what I live for.

When I told some of my "family" of the things that were happening, medically, and the reason behind writing this book, I heard concern and worry. I heard denial. I heard jokes to lighten the mood. I heard optimism. I heard hope. I heard faith. All of those things told me my family loves me.

All I want is for all of them to be happy in their life, but that I can't control it. I can still have faith. All I want is for them to have memories for their future.

I've been blessed by the remarkable amount of support from all of my family. How blessed my life has been, since I've seen the soft, sheer tent cover me to show that I'm encompassed by safety and comfort.

Today, I left my house to be out with a friend for a little while. My little girl cried and cried because she said she would miss me so much even though I'd only be gone for a short time. When I got home after being out, the first thing I saw was my husband. Then my wee lass came running toward me, with her little cheeks red from taking a nap. My son had taken a nap as well and had asked why I was gone for so long. When I realized I don't go out and do things for myself a lot, coming home was such a wonderful feeling. I was greeted like I mattered.

Through my life, there have been times when I've felt routine. When you fall into routine is when things become mundane and repetitive. I was only out of my routine for four hours and I felt like a new person. Holding onto my family, after being away for that short time, was a gift. I was also able to spend time with my niece today and it was that much more special. The whole night, I felt loved and I felt like my love was overflowing for everyone around me.

Routine can sometimes be a good thing. It means things can be stable in your life right now. It doesn't mean nothing is important. It just means to hold onto those moments with your family more because, for right now, it's at peace.

"There's no vocabulary for love within a family,
love that's lived in but not looked at, love within
the light of which all else is seen, the love within
which all other love finds speech. This love is silent."
–T.S. Eliot

♥ 23 ♥

Husband

I broke these discussions of family up into categories. I've already discussed friendships and wanted to also encompass them into the family category with my biological family. I've said all of this to you before. I will say it again because I want this to be written for whomever else reads this. I write all of this so I'm writing out a piece of me. If you gain insight for yourself, it's great. If you don't, just as well. These are my experiences and lessons I've learned and wanted to share with you. This chapter is much more personal. This entire chapter is dedicated solely to my marriage to, Matt.

Our marriage, our life together these years, has taught me love does conquer all. It's been proven from the moment of our vows. We have had such strife at times, a lot of anger, a whole lot of tests of patience, and tests in general, but so much love.

Husband

Sometimes it's been fierce love which wasn't always a good thing.

I appreciate our relationship and our respect for each other. What he's given me is something that I never thought could be real. There is no "perfect" anyone. It's such a fairytale. It never stays the way the movie ends. It's not a plot where you have one issue with each other and then it's one big happy end to a perfect movie with people who have amazing bodies. I'm not going to lie, I'm sitting here looking like a blob writing this and somehow he loves me anyways.

The thing about our marriage I've appreciated most of all, even though it wasn't in our vows, both of us have never called each other names and we've never said we've hated each other. I think it's a huge accomplishment with how things are in this generation. We've both been very angry and we still never name called or said the horrid "hate" word. It has shown me how much of an example we are setting for our kids, and I just want that for other people. I want others to know that they can accept to be loved the way we love each other. Name calling and using the word hate, are both so destructive and accomplish nothing in any type of resolution of a conflict.

"Let's not forget it's you and me versus the problem. Not you versus me." –Steve Maraboli

To Matt, thank you for being a partner with me, to set that boundary with.

Technically, today is our 12th wedding anniversary. So this chapter is even more perfect than what I had originally planned to write.

The day before our anniversary, in 2010, was the day that we lost our baby we hadn't even known about. I would never wish that pain for anyone. I loved the support he gave me. I knew he was in pain about it, even though he was just trying to be the steady rock against my crashing waves of tears. That moment changed our entire lives. We hadn't known it yet, but it did.

When we found out about the tumor, he was the first one with me through everything. He was the one holding my hand and telling me no matter what, we'd be okay.

One of the hardest days was having our talk about the seriousness of everything that could happen and what we needed to plan for if it did. I still hate talking about it. I hate the thought of not being able to be with him.

I remember a dream I had years ago. I was walking in a driveway and my phone started ringing. I picked up the phone and they said he had died. I remember crashing to my knees and letting out a blood curdling scream and staring at the sky with my arms outstretched. I screamed and sobbed all in one breath.

I know this can never feel to you all reading this, or for Matt, the way it felt for me, since it was all in my head. I just want to say that is how much I love him. I would fall to my knees and I would feel like somehow, my heart would stop beating and I would have no air left in my lungs. I've loved him so hard and in such an incredible way, and it's grown since, I don't know how I would live life without him. I know I would have to for our kids. I just know it would be so much more painful.

To everyone else who is reading this, please understand love. Not lust or disillusionment. Love is not something that just happens and you decide one day you just can't do it anymore. A relationship is built on a foundation of compatible **friendship**, first, and foremost. Marriage is a commitment to your partner that you would be there no matter what. That's not just an "until". It was a promise. People spout out how "marriage is hard work". They never say anything other than that. No elaboration. I've found the real "work" in marriage is while you're growing up together, you must continue to learn how to love and support each other through that process. Putting it like that sounds so incredibly difficult. So many marriages are failing. Having kids, especially, is a huge strain on a marriage. Lack of sleep, long hours, trying to juggle so many other things, falling into a routine; you barely find a way to make room for each other. I know. We've all done it.

When I got home today, I hugged my husband. I don't know why I felt like I'd never felt his hug before. It felt so safe and real. I was so thankful for it.

Thank you to my Matty, whom I love, cherish, fight, glare, and insanely fall for you each and every day. You make so many days worth every second. I will forever be grateful of May 27th, when you asked me to marry you. It's been a crazy ride. It has been anything but boring and we're always on our toes. Even though we don't have the same love language, I'm glad you still give me hearts and flowers when I ask or when you know I need it most. You are a wonderful companion and my best friend.

"Even when the light is dull and the room dark
and dreary,

HeARTwork

My mind fills easier with hope and peace just by
having you lay near me.
The road this trip has taken, is not what
we'd foreseen,
And sometimes it's hard and painful to keep saying
'what will be, will be'.
The chances, outcomes, and risks always seem to
filter through,
But in the odds of those outcomes, the changes are
easier to accept with you."
-Kiyomi's Broken Brain

To my life, my love, and my dear, "Like now".

♥Aunty Anne♥

HeARTwork

What can I even say about my NTN (aunty Anne)? I honestly have no idea how to even describe someone such as her. When we are around each other, it's like thoughts have no meaning! Either we're laughing too hard or we can tell what the other is thinking. She has a "gift" too. I'm able to talk to her a lot about things since it's very mutual and we can understand it. Since she moved to Scotland, I don't get to see her often. She and my Uncle Ray have visited a few times since they've moved. The last time I saw her was when she came between being diagnosed with the brain tumor and before I had the surgery. It was the best gift to have during that time. I remember the day she had to leave our house. I knew neither of us wanted to talk about her leaving until the very second we had to say goodbye. When she needed to go, my body had no hold over my contorted ugly crying face and the tears pouring out. I didn't want to let her go. I didn't want to watch her go. She "gets" me. Some of my favorite laughs I remember are with her. I've never wanted to be with her more than now.

1. What was your happiest moment as a child? As an adult?

Seaside holidays were my happiest moments, as a child. I felt so free and at peace, with the five of us, together.. It was very difficult to go home again.
As an adult, moving to Portland was bitter-sweet. It was a new beginning and I realized I

was capable of surviving, on my own. That was a magical feeling, of accomplishment.

2. What›s the most beautiful thing you›ve ever witnessed? What is the most beautiful thing you could give to someone else?

The delighted look on my sweet dogs' faces, when they had a litter of new puppies, was tender and hear melting and utterly beautiful. The most beautiful thing I can give is my time and support, even if it's to my old dog. Un-rushed attention is a valuable gift.

3. What makes you feel wealthy in life or love?

The feeling that someone treasures and adores me makes me feel wealthy. I'm very lucky. What could you add to your life that would make you more wealthy than you already are? A winning lottery ticket. One could make a lot of people happy, with a jackpot win.

♥ 24 ♥

Kids

I have to let you know something, before we get into talking about kids. It's more of a story really, I guess.

When I was 18, my mom, Matt, and I were in the outpatient surgery at the hospital. I was prepped and ready for the operation and we were awaiting the go ahead from the gynecologist. He came in and discussed that I had a large complex cyst on my right ovary. He reminded us I'd be having the cyst removed, but because of how large it was and the position, they weren't sure if they were going to be able to save my ovary. I remember my mom quietly and modestly pleading for the best he could do to save it.

When I awoke and was in recovery, the doctor came in to let us know all of the information from what had happened. He was able to save the ovary, and then there was the "but". He told me that if I ever wanted children or was ever able to have them, I would need to have them at a young age. Looking back, I can't quite remember the reasoning in medical terminology. He left quickly after that point and my mom and I cried. I looked over toward Matt and used my eyes as some sort of an apology. Honestly, I don't think it was the fact that it was the news. I think that my mom and I had already prepared for that outcome from the age of 15 or a little before, from all of the menstrual issues, including polycystic ovarian syndrome and endometriosis. I think it was that it had been confirmed at that point. It was said out loud by a professional and reality had set in, in a very harsh way.

I knew I wanted children. Matt was told he couldn't have children when he was 17. I was just told at 18 that I may not be able to have children. After several years of marriage, it just became something that we came to terms with, that adopting would be the route we'd need to take if we decided on children.

It wasn't until I was 24, after five years of marriage; we both realized the possibility of having a child would be real. I had had a miscarriage without knowing it, the day before our anniversary. In a still moment of something so incredibly painful, shocking, and gut throbbing, there was a moment of faith realized. We both knew at that point that we wanted to try and have a baby. It took us ten months of fertility treatments to finally have a positive pregnancy test. That was with our son.

He was our rainbow. The vibrant of beautiful when light breaks through the storm.

We had made the idea we would be fine with just one, since he was a blessing. They had explained that we would have to go through the whole process to conceive again to insure a viable pregnancy. Then BAM! In one of the most trying times of our marriage, I found out I was pregnant. Scared is not even a word I would use to describe the feeling I had before seeing the first ultrasound. I was preparing myself for a complete disaster inside and outside of my uterus. Then, there was this tiny little bean that had a beautiful and steady heartbeat.

"It's a girl. Anything that fights this hard to be here, in our family, is always a girl." That is what my Aunty Anne said on the phone, when I told her the news. She was right. Kimie, named after my maternal grandmother from Japan, is our "heart of gold" little girl. We had found our rainbow and the pot of gold at the end.

Parenting on the other hand, needs crash course in school!

Being honest like I promised I would be, I've been having such a different attitude toward my parenting since the night that Kimie needed to be held. Even though things looked differently from surgery, medications can take a huge toll on a person, especially when they are steroids or sedative medications.

When my attitude changed, my kid's attitude changed as well. I haven't worried about the house looking pristine. I haven't worried about cleaning before someone comes over. Actually, it had been to the point that if someone was coming down the driveway, my daughter would yell, "HURRY!" throughout the house while picking up things from the living room and dining room, really anywhere where their things were spread about.

I'm sure, as parents, we go through the thought of being a good parent. I've questioned it more since surgery than I've ever had. Even though I knew I wanted children, and I had my beautiful kids, questioning every move you make is tiring.

I wonder all of the time how I'm ruining my kids. My son had said a few times that he missed the "before mommy". I can't tell you how many hours I've spent in my bathroom sobbing. There are things that happen and it's like a kick to my gut. I sit in my bathroom and silently cry about how much I'm ruining them and if they would be better off without being around me. It's a huge pity party in my toilet room no one else is invited. Sometimes I get in the shower and cry, mainly because there is more sound surrounding the bathroom. I only save the shower cries for the direst days.

I have those days more and more, where I cry about my kids. It can happen at any time, really. Sometimes it's when I feel like I should just leave the picture and give them an opportunity that they may not be able to have because of the situation I've put us in. Other times it's because they are doing something so precious and I don't want to leave them. Just a moment ago, they were playing a singing competition. They'd each stand in the middle of the room, their little heads held so high, and sing a made up song, or sometimes throw in a familiar one. The one not singing "on stage", would be sitting in front of the other, then I'd hear the queue of applause and cheering. That moment can never really be explained to someone else. It's a moment of sadness, joy, heart-warming, heartache, love, and being proud.

We have days where we ask each other what we appreciate or love about our family. It's nice to hear your kid's point of view about how they view their family and home life. The following quotes, are what my children have said to me.

"I love you because you're my mommy and you love my heart and you're kind. I love you because you are respectful and that you make me so, so happy." Kimie's descriptions are always broken down into finer detail.

"I love you because you love people and you're special. You love people and it doesn't matter who they are." Leighlan is much more rounded in descriptions.

They both said even though I've had my head cut open, I'm just different but still the same. I was worried because of the "before mommy" comment, they would feel responsible for things. Leighlan said they don't worry about me, they just miss me when they go somewhere for a while. I had asked what they think about my "headaches". They said that they don't really think about it and just like to bring ice packs because they are big helpers.

I think the thing that blew me away the most was the response to my question of how all of this has changed them or us. This was Leighlan's response to the question.

"We all change. We get bigger and grow up. You only changed because you have a cut in your head and sometimes need medicine to stop seizures. You know what mom? I change every day and so does Kimie. You have a cut in your head and sometimes people stare at your eyebrow and eyelashes but you have a lot of love in your heart and that's what matters forever."

Through this whole thing, I feel like it sounds horrible to say, they have kept me headstrong. It makes me think that I rely on them to get me through. I know I hear parents say all the time if it weren't for their kids, they don't know how they would've gotten through. It really is true.

This Mother's Day, my kids were so upset that the day was only about celebrating mothers. We talked to them about how when kids get older, they start to understand why appreciating those days, like Mother's Day and Father's Day, are important. We told them it's not about gifts, it's about appreciating the love and attention that was given by our parents throughout our lives.

This Mother's Day was very different, though. Only three days after Mother's Day, I was having a hysterectomy. I'm 31 years old. The reality of only having Leighlan six years ago and having Kimie four years ago, made me feel like I was so blessed. In those six years, I had a son, a daughter, a brain tumor, a brain surgery, and almost two years of undiagnosed seizures. Blessed. So, this Mother's Day, I did celebrate them. I told them I never knew I could feel so happy and blessed, all because of the timing of their arrival. We planned to have Leighlan. Kimie just fought her way through before everything else happened. She came only one year before the brain tumor was found.

"To my baby,

Whoever you may be, whoever you may come to be, know you are loved. My life is now your life and your life, mine. You will forever be in my heart and I will care and love you indefinitely.

My sweet child. My dream for you is to grow healthy and know equality. I dream you educate your mind to as much possibility as you can. I dream you know the difference between your head and your heart. Find a person who shares your morals and values above anything else. I dream your life is full of happiness and that you go through life not worrying about small things. Know the difference between what's important and what's not.

Most of all, I dream for you to be a person who cares and stands up for what they believe in. My mother, your grandmother, always told me, "Do what you can in this moment. If you can't change it, don't worry about it until you can."

I've wanted and loved you before I even knew you to exist. Please find yourself and know that no matter who or what you choose to be, we love you." –Kiyomi before children

I gave them life, through birth. However, they give me life by being my reason to live.

♥ 25 ♥

Focus

Soon after surgery, and after we realized no one was helping me, I was battling terrible constant pain. It's hard to keep your mind away from the pain and focus on the rest of what is around you. People with chronic pain will understand. I felt like I needed a distraction.

I made a comment to Matt about how I would love to have a camera to use for photography. Mind you, I've never had classes or have ever had a camera that was anything but one of those little ones you keep in your purse for instant moments.

Matt and I were walking through a store and he saw a camera bundle he thought would be a good idea. I was hesitant because of the price, but with pain, you do anything to try and alleviate it in any sort of way.

By nine months of having my camera, people were asking if I'd be willing to do photos for them. Never did I realize this would be such a huge pivot point in my life and in my mindset.

I began doing photos for people and it would help tremendously for a distraction. I would get the distraction from the actual session and then an additional distraction with the editing process. This was also before the seizures were much more regular, as well.

I was beginning to schedule photos regularly for people. I didn't want to use props, I'd decided. I felt like every person is beautiful and I didn't want the photos to take away from their beauty. I wanted each person's personality to shine through each photo. Before the actual sessions, I would get to know the family and hear everything they wanted and gather how they like to do things.

My focus became other people and how they see life and how they see themselves. Most everyone was so self conscious. They all had a weakness they saw about themselves. We all do, but it baffled me it was so collective among people who were going to be photographed. We are so self-depreciating

Not only were the photos booking up, I started realizing my actual passion about photography. Most of the time, I would hear about how fat they felt, or how they didn't want a certain body part to show.

Now, before I go into realizing my passion, let me explain the choice of name for my photography. I call it "Happy Beautiful Wealthy". My grandmother, Kimie, had written my name in Japanese in a way it represented happy, beautiful, and wealthy. I decided in honor of her, and in honor of how I wanted to see myself and life prosper, this would be the best name decision.

Focus

I began to do a session called "HBW". I would ask people to nominate who they felt represented Happy, Beautiful, and Wealthy. The nominated person would be a featured person with their photo shoot. I gave them questions to answer for being represented. My goal was to try and have people dig deep into their inner selves and think about their life in a positive light. The people you've read about in this book, are only a very small amount I've been able to get to know.

This became the focus. I became enthralled with people who would answer the questions. It was amazing to hear every person's answers because they were all different. I loved hearing about their lives and what they found in their perception to emanate what they believed or wanted.

Our focus as a family changed as well. Our kids became so involved with wanting to give to others. They wanted to raise money or donations for things that meant a great deal to them. It made me so proud they were seeing others in a different light rather than the normalcy of what's happening in the world.

Through photography, I've met people from all walks of life. I've even made friends with strangers who I've kept in touch with. I've loved learning about their lives. When I post the feature of the person on my photography page, their friends or family get to read about how they've perceived their life and point of view and even learn something new about them. It's such a wonderful thing to see how supportive and loving everyone can become to each other.

All of the focus that was on all of the pain I was trying to endure was, instead, put onto people who were beautiful and wonderful to get to know. This has changed my heart in a way I don't know how to express. It's as if my heart has grown, like you've exercised and your muscles get bigger and then add in a light surrounding it. I am constantly surrounded by all of these happy, beautiful, and wealthy people. I'm able to have an opportunity to talk to someone new and hear about their life. My favorite stranger meet up was at a McDonald's. My nephew and I had been done with a friend's wedding and we stopped for a bite to eat. I met a lovely couple who were about to celebrate their 50th wedding anniversary. I couldn't pass up a chance to speak to them and get to know them.

I think the biggest twist through all of this, the focus has become seeing the beautiful in everything, even through pain.

HeARTwork

1. What was your favorite memory as a child? As an adult?

My favorite memory when I was a child was having so many adventures. It's funny to think back now, especially since I'm older, that most of our family adventures were cheap thrills since our family didn't have a lot of money. One memory in particular, even though it scared the shit out of me, was after we watched the movie "E.T" together as a family. I was probably around seven years old. My mom and step dad (dad) decided it would be such a great idea to have all of us go searching for that stupid alien. Everyone else was on board. I remember Dad showing us gravel that was disturbed and said it was the alien's footprints. We then went to a local park, in the dark, and were using flashlights to check around again, for the stupid alien. All of a sudden, I heard this loud crunching noise and I screamed and ran back to our vehicle. When I found out what it was, Dad had thrown Reese's Pieces on the ground and that's what I had stepped on.

My favorite memory as an adult, so far, has been the birth of both children. Having to sort through all of the wonderful moments as an adult is a hard thing to do. However, both births were extremely stressful and both ended up in emergency c-sections. Being able to see their faces and hear their voices now reminds me of the time where having that future could have been taken away from us so quickly.

2. What is the most beautiful thing you've ever witnessed? What is the most beautiful thing you can give to someone else?

The most beautiful thing that I have ever witnessed has been love. When I've seen love in the face of death, birth, passionate anger, in unbiased acceptance, it's the most amazing thing to witness. I get really upset when some judgmental religious people use Love as a weapon. They say it out of trying to sound superior. It makes me really upset because that isn't real Love. Real Love isn't just a deep regard for someone. Love is practicing true acceptance without any expectation of change. Love from a distance if you have to. You can always change the direction of your love as people change.

The most beautiful thing I can give to someone else is Love and Time. Especially time. A friend and I were in a discussion about how she wasn't going to be able to make a meeting with me and two other clients. She needed to be with a friend who is terminal. Her friend was invited to speak to a college about dealing with terminal illness. She was apologizing about needing to change plans and such. I stopped her right in her tracks. It doesn't matter even if it was about that she just wanted to spend some time on her couch. Never apologize for any time that is yours. Every person's time is precious. If you don't want to do something, don't agree to it and don't do it. This is your time. You won't get that back. It's a treasure to give out. When you give time, it should be for or out of love. So, Love and Time are the most beautiful things I could give to someone else. Especially when you have time threatened to you.

3. What makes you feel wealthy in life and love? What could you add to your life that can make you feel wealthier than you already have now?

My family makes me feel wealthy. I have an abundance of wealthy, actually. I feel blessed everyday to wake up and have the children I have and a husband who I know is always here for me. The discussions that happen in our home are all about learning and how to change the world we live in, in a positive way. I am wealthy in a way I never thought I could be. It's the riches of happiness, beauty of the world, and wealth of knowledge that make me think of sitting in a Buddhist garden listening to the steady wind and wooden chimes around, to provide the Zen within life.

I could add meeting more people and inviting more love into my life. I love the knowledge of listening to other's lives. It's amazing, even just a person who you love most has a completely different take on life than your own. The person sitting next to you at a bus stop has a life that you don't even know where it's been. Remember, every memory is singular. Every perspective is different, even if the same action happens in front of several people. Each one

Focus

will have a different account of life. It's amazing to have an abundance of perceptions. You may learn something you hadn't thought of before.

♥ 26 ♥

Time

The dreaded Father Time was the very last on my list and the one I've had to prep for myself.

All of our lives are based on time. Every single aspect revolves around it. Time for us starts when our mothers are waiting for us to arrive, then time rushes us to grow up. It wakes us up in the morning, it puts us to bed at night, it dictates our conversations and how we spend our days. Time runs our entire life. We have holidays or birthdays we look forward to, key word being forward. We wait for things to come, and wave goodbye to things that have gone.

Imagine standing on the top of a hill. You're able to look out at the cityscape that seems to bow at your feet. Imagine staying still on that hilltop and watching the horizon like a movie. They fast-forward the night to day and day to night, repeating the cycle continuously, even moving through the seasons. All while you're still standing there motionless. This imagery is what I envision for the saying "time passes you by" or "time flies by". I think I imagine it this way because it's what I'd want to see, apart from the moon and sun setting repeatedly within seconds, I would stand on the hilltop and try to halt time. No matter what, it brushes away like a gust of wind. Seasons change, landscapes change, clouds change, sunsets change, people change, their faces change, and while we can't seem to see past that small bit of horizon, the world is changing.

Our time here is so little. Not just for us individually but for the family before us and the family after us. I try to imagine life when my great grandmother lived. I try to place myself in a time that I wish I could have known. We truly, will never know it all. No matter how many studies are done or historians try and decipher from the past, we will never know it all. This day in age, we will have the capacity to know what life was and is like from this generation. We have actually made time, if you think about it. We have made time so that there isn't something to question in the future. We have video and photos that show how stupid we've become or how beautiful kindness can be. We have only a limited amount of time to make our life documented in a way that can be used for learning, for love, for kindness, for our families, for support, and for our future.

Time is always taken away from us, is how some people see it. You know that "is the glass half empty or half full" saying? What if you thought of time in that sense? Is our time taken away from us or given to us? Any amount of time given to me is time I can either waste or time I can choose to appreciate. I love time with my family and experiencing life with others in a way shows the world, love. I'm thankful for all of the time I'm given. I'm thankful for the time I've used, even unwisely. I'm thankful for the time I've spent being able to write this down and so thankful for you giving your time to read it.

Time takes away from our bodies providing us with age. However, Time will never take away your ability to love, give kindness, or to imperfect all of...

Your heARTwork.

❤ Acknowledgments ❤

My momma gave so much inspiration for this book. She was the best first teacher I could have never thought to have asked for. "Momma's always right." My dad gave me the laughter I've needed to continue through this life, instead of puckering my lips like a butthole from being too-sour-a-lemon-about-life.

To all of my siblings, step, adopted, and birthed, we were the original laughter makers and the test subjects to Dad's undying humor.

I want to give appreciation to every HBW person who allowed me to write them into this book. Thank you so much for giving your time and allowing us to see the beauty of your life.

I would love to name every one of my friends and family, but I have entirely too many. I love you and appreciate every single one of you who have given me support and believed in this project. It's been a long road, not just with the book.

To Shannon: I cannot express the immense thanks for reading this book time after time. Not only did you give your time to me, but you helped shape this book from description to order. I can honestly say, I don't remember how many times you had to read through this and never gave me grief. Thank you so much.

To Alicia: You were my reading test subject. The positivity you had about this book, gave me the confidence to keep going. Also, implementing the "Hedy Method" helped immensely and brought this book further into life.

To Hedy: I hope I've done well enough to meet your standards. Please don't make me stand in front of the class to give a report.

Aunty Anne and Uncle Ray, you both have been my cheerleaders from Scotland. Imagine, all those times we've wanted to scream at those doctors, has led to something like this!

To Leighlan and Kimie. I was given the most amazing gift of being able to have you as my children. Your warm hearts and charismatic personalities make everyday special and serve as a constant reminder there is always something good in a day.

Nate, you were always patient with me and helped me learn new and different things. I don't know, truly, if any of this would have come to how it has, without you being a huge part in it. Thank you. I love you big brother.

Just because you're last, does not make you the least important. Matty, you have given me so much more than I can ever think to put into words. One of them is support. You've been supportive through the good and bad. You've pushed me to be better and have pushed me to madness. The good and the bad, the great and the horrible, the anguish and the triumph, has all been with you. Thank you for standing by my side as an equal, standing in front of me as a

Acknowledgments

protector, and standing behind me to encourage me to move forward. I have loved you in this life and I am fortunate to be the one to do so.

Lightning Source UK Ltd.
Milton Keynes UK
UKHW041518250722
406336UK00003B/831

9 781545 672235